Ancient Africa

Discovering Lost Stories from Africa's Early Civilizations

© Copyright 2025 - All rights reserved.

The content contained within this book may not be reproduced, duplicated, or transmitted without direct written permission from the author or the publisher.

Under no circumstances will any blame or legal responsibility be held against the publisher, or author, for any damages, reparation, or monetary loss due to the information contained within this book, either directly or indirectly.

Legal Notice:

This book is copyright protected. It is only for personal use. You cannot amend, distribute, sell, use, quote, or paraphrase any part, or the content within this book, without the consent of the author or publisher.

Disclaimer Notice:

Please note the information contained within this document is for educational and entertainment purposes only. All effort has been executed to present accurate, up-to-date, reliable, and complete information. No warranties of any kind are declared or implied. Readers acknowledge that the author is not engaging in the rendering of legal, financial, medical, or professional advice. The content within this book has been derived from various sources. Please consult a licensed professional before attempting any techniques outlined in this book.

By reading this document, the reader agrees that under no circumstances is the author responsible for any losses, direct or indirect, that are incurred as a result of the use of the information contained within this document, including, but not limited to, errors, omissions, or inaccuracies.

Free Bonus from Captivating History (Available for a Limited time)

Hi History Lovers!

Now you have a chance to join our exclusive history list so you can get your first history ebook for free as well as discounts and a potential to get more history books for free!

Simply visit the link below to join.

Or, Scan the QR code!

captivatinghistory.com/ebook

Also, make sure to follow us on Facebook, X, and YouTube by searching for Captivating History.

Table of Contents

INTRODUCTION 1
CHAPTER 1 - LOST KINGDOMS OF THE NILE: KERMA, KUSH, AND BEYOND 3
CHAPTER 2 - THE MYSTERIOUS LAND OF PUNT: MYTHS AND REALITIES 18
CHAPTER 3 - NOK AND THE DAWN OF ANCIENT NIGERIA 31
CHAPTER 4 - THE SAN AND THE EARLY TRIBES OF AFRICA 41
CHAPTER 5 - CARTHAGE BEYOND HANNIBAL 53
CHAPTER 6 - THE LOST TRIBES OF THE SAHARA DESERT 65
CHAPTER 7 - ANCIENT BERBER KINGDOMS: NUMIDIA AND MAURETANIA 73
CHAPTER 8 - FORGOTTEN EMPIRES OF LATE ANTIQUITY: AXUM AND DJENNÉ-DJENNO 87
CHAPTER 9 - ENIGMATIC RUINS AND MYTHICAL CITIES OF ANCIENT AFRICA 99
CONCLUSION 111
HERE'S ANOTHER BOOK BY MATT CLAYTON THAT YOU MIGHT LIKE 113
FREE BONUS FROM CAPTIVATING HISTORY (AVAILABLE FOR A LIMITED TIME) 114
BIBLIOGRAPHY 115
IMAGE SOURCES 118

Introduction

Whenever people think of ancient Africa, their minds immediately leap to ancient Egypt. And that makes sense; with all of its towering pyramids, legendary pharaohs, and grand temples, Egypt was one of the greatest civilizations of the ancient world and the main star of African history. Yet, the kingdom's fame cast a long shadow over the rest of the continent. Africa was home to diverse people and cultures. The Sahara has been inhabited by many innovative tribes centuries ago.

While many may picture the Sahara as nothing more than endless sand and rocks, the desert has not always been that way. Thousands of years ago, the Sahara was very different from what we see today. It was much greener and filled with rivers and lakes that could sustain a mix of both people and animals. People who settled across the Sahara during these times thrived. They fished in the rivers, hunted in the plains, and built organized communities. It was only when the climate changed that the land dried, becoming the Sahara that we know today. The rivers vanished, and the grasslands turned to dunes, leading to a few societies fading away.

However, this change did not obliterate every single living being there. There were still those who found ways to live and prosper. Despite the desert seeming uninhabitable, these people managed to establish trade networks, turning the dry region into a bustling center of commerce and cultural exchange.

This colorful scene was not only limited to the Sahara. In West Africa, the Nok civilization rose to prominence. Although its history was briefly lost, covered by the sands of time, the discovery of their peculiar terracotta sculpture brought the civilization back into the spotlight. To the south of the Sahara was the city of Djenné-Djenno, which was known for its markets and agriculture. The Kingdom of Axum—also referred to as the Axumite Empire—lay farther east. Despite its mysterious origins, the kingdom went on to become a force to be reckoned with, especially after spreading its influence across the Arabian Peninsula.

Then, there were stories of the Kushites and the Carthaginians. These two African civilizations are often remembered for their clashes with Egypt and Rome, although they were powerful in their own right. The Kushites had a rich heritage and cultural identity despite being heavily influenced by the Egyptians. Interestingly, there was a period when Egypt was ruled by Kushite pharaohs, though historical accounts often reduce them to rivals of the Egyptians. Carthage suffered a similar fate. Since the Carthaginian Empire's stories come mostly from their conquerors, Carthage is frequently portrayed as the villain in Roman histories.

Just as Africa's landscapes stretch from the barren deserts to the lush rainforests, mountains, and savannahs, the continent's history is equally expansive and varied. From the Garamantes, who invented underground irrigation systems in the Sahara, to the San, the masters of hunting and poison, this book aims to look into the lesser-known stories of ancient Africa.

Chapter 1 – Lost Kingdoms of the Nile: Kerma, Kush, and Beyond

Egypt may be the first kingdom that pops into our minds whenever we think about the world's oldest civilizations. It was a rich kingdom in terms of both wealth and history. The story of pharaohs spanned from around 3100 BCE (though these kings were not referred to as pharaohs until around 1400 BCE) when the lands were first united to 30 BCE when it finally fell to Rome. However, beyond these well-worn pathways of ancient Egypt and along the same winding Nile lay a few other kingdoms whose names are nowhere near as popular as Egypt. Despite being categorized as "lesser-known kingdoms," these realms have equally compelling histories.

Ta-Seti, for example, was a kingdom whose story stretched back to an era that predated even the founding of Egypt. Believe it or not, Ta-Seti's people were already thriving in Nubia, what is today northern Sudan and southern Egypt, long before Egypt's first pharaoh united the land to the north. As more artifacts were uncovered, such as palace ruins, hieroglyphs, and a crown, scholars began to debate that Ta-Seti might have been the oldest ancient monarchy to ever exist. Based on a few findings, the first kings of Ta-Seti might have begun to rule around 5900 BCE.

Ta-Seti was the name given to the kingdom by the Egyptians themselves. It meant the "Land of the Bow" since the kingdom was believed to be the home to skilled archers. Yes, even the Egyptians recognized the reputation of Ta-Seti's warriors. They were equally feared and respected for their mastery of the bow. At times, they were used as mercenaries, but there were also times when the Ta-Seti archers were formidable opponents of the Egyptians.

The Nile was extremely precious to those who inhabited the lands close to it. Since the people of Ta-Seti built their society close to the river's edge, they were blessed with an abundance of agricultural resources. The silt-laden soil nourished their many crops, which included barley, emmer wheat, and a diverse variety of vegetables. This land, which was made fertile by the annual flooding of the Nile, fed the people and allowed the kingdom to flourish.

Of course, agriculture was not the only source of Ta-Seti's wealth. The land was also rich with deposits of gold and copper. These natural resources and the kingdom's prime location, which bridged northern Egypt and the lands beyond Nubia, let Ta-Seti thrive as a vital trading post. It is plausible that caravan trails and trade routes once snaked through the landscape, stretching into lands of other ancient civilizations where traders would exchange gold, ivory, and incense, to name a few sought-after goods. Artisan works like intricate jewelry and ceremonial items were also highly sought after among the traders who found themselves in Ta-Seti. These goods would eventually find their way into Egyptian temples and palaces.

An aerial view of irrigation from the Nile River.[1]

The kingdom's spiritual life was also complex and rich. The most important deities worshiped by the people were known as Heru, Auset (the goddess Isis), and Khnum. These gods were central to Ta-Seti's spiritual practices. While the falcon-headed god Heru was often depicted in symbols of protection and kingship, the deity was also held in high regard by Ta-Seti's warriors. Auset, on the other hand, was thought to be the embodiment of fertility and magic. She was best known for her nurturing and powerful motherly presence. Meanwhile, Khnum, the ram-headed god, watched over the Nile. These deities eventually became the central figures in the Egyptian pantheon, proving Ta-Seti's influence on Egyptian religion and culture. Heru was turned into Horus, and Auset became the goddess Isis. Khnum, however, retained his name and was hailed as one of the Egyptians' earliest gods. The ancient Egyptians believed Khnum was responsible for shaping humanity on his potter's wheel.

A depiction of Khnum (in the middle) carved onto the wall of a temple in Esna, Egypt.*

Unlike other popular ancient civilizations such as Rome or even Greece, the people of Ta-Seti held women in high regard. There has been evidence that women once wore the mantle as leaders in Ta-Seti. Also known as Kentake (referred to as Candace by the Romans) or "Queen Mother," these women held power in their own right, perhaps embodying the protective spirit of the goddess Auset. Egypt also saw female pharaohs ascend to the throne. Perhaps the ancient Egyptians had been influenced by Ta-Seti in this regard as well.

Of course, as time went by, Ta-Seti's influence waned, replaced by the rising power of Egypt. Some scholars suggest that Ta Seti's rulers might have played a role in the unification of Egypt—either through conquest or alliances. Ta-Seti was eventually integrated into the Egyptian kingdom, becoming the first-ever nome. It served as a significant administrative and military center.

Ta-Seti's culture and beliefs shaped Egypt's early religious and social structures. Ta-Seti's royal symbols, artifacts, and even gods became intertwined with Egyptian culture. Its influence persisted in the temples dotted across Egypt and in the kingdom's colorful art and mythology. Perhaps it was because of this gradual integration into Egyptian culture that the story of Ta-Seti is often overshadowed by that of Egypt.

Kerma, a Nubian Kingdom That Egypt Envied

The history of Kerma first reached the public in the 20th century. In the 1920s, archaeologists made a massive discovery along the Nile's curve in modern-day northern Sudan. Here, they unearthed the remnants of an ancient city known as Kerma that once thrived thousands of years prior. Upon research, early scholars were able to arrive at a conclusion: they believed Kerma was either a base or a fort managed by Egyptian governors who served under the pharaoh.

However, this conclusion soon changed when archaeologists discovered more artifacts and royal burial sites that proved otherwise. It was crystal clear that Kerma was not merely an Egyptian fort. In fact, Kerma was an independent kingdom with its own authority. Its reputation was further cemented when scholars got their hands on Egyptian records dated from the Middle Kingdom. In these texts, the Egyptians described a powerful kingdom that existed in an area south of Egypt, particularly in the region of ancient Nubia—the same region where Kerma stood—which they referred to as Kush.

What remains of the city of Kerma.[3]

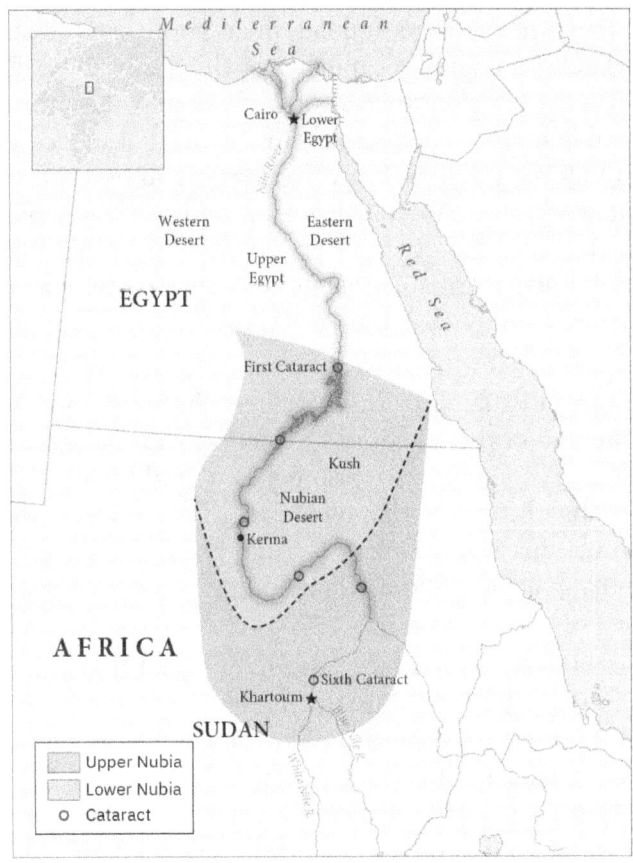

Map of Nubia, including Kerma.[4]

Given Kerma's strategic location along vital caravan routes, linking Egypt to sub-Saharan Africa, the Red Sea, and the Horn of Africa, it is not surprising that Kerma was considered the focal point of traders from all over the continent. The city thrived as a bustling hub of trade. Apart from common goods such as agricultural products and precious metals, Kerma played a crucial role in the trade of luxury items and exotic animals.

Knowing how vital the kingdom's role was in trade activities, especially for merchants transporting luxury goods from the central African interior to Egypt, the people of Kerma made sure their responsibilities were not limited to being only participants in the trade. Since Kerma was perfectly positioned at the impassable Third Cataract along the Nile, the people of Kerma made sure to firmly control the flow of trade.

Upon nearing Kerma, merchants who had been navigating the Nile had no other choice but to unload their goods and continue their journey overland. Once in the capital city, which was also called Kerma, merchants had to register their goods. By doing this, the people of Kerma were able to keep track of valuable items that moved across their territory and enforce taxation. Since Kerma was an essential stop on the Nile trade network, these merchants would redirect their valuable items to the city, further adding to Kerma's coffers. This control over commerce solidified Kerma's reputation as a powerful and resourceful kingdom.

As the kingdom grew even wealthier, the leaders of Kerma became more ambitious in expanding their frontiers. From about 1700 to 1500 BCE, near the end of the kingdom's existence, Kerma began showing its teeth. No longer content with just being a trade hub, the kingdom attempted to absorb neighboring territories. The Sudanese Kingdom of Sai, for example, became a part of Kerma. From a booming trade hub, Kerma eventually turned into a sizable empire, controlling a substantial stretch of the Nile.

With this growth in territory, Kerma's population swelled. More urban centers emerged, and artisans, merchants, and warriors played a role in contributing to the kingdom's wealth. Despite starting off as a kingdom of agriculture and trade, Kerma's military might was indeed impressive. Based on archaeological discoveries, scholars are confident that the leaders of Kerma often focused on the kingdom's defense. As a rapidly rising power in the region, Kerma's wealth helped the people build more military infrastructures. The capital city itself had grand fortifications made out of mudbrick to repel invasions and attacks.

When it comes to architecture, the most iconic example of Kerma's innovation is known as the Deffufa, a tall mudbrick structure. The Western Deffufa stood at least eighteen meters tall. This temple-like structure was unlike anything seen in Egypt or possibly anywhere else. It featured columned rooms, passageways, paintings, and a shrine. Although its exact purpose is debated, most scholars believe it was once a religious center. Excavations revealed the remains of a limestone altar, which further supports the suggestion that the structure might have been used for rituals, particularly animal sacrifices.

The Western Deffufa.⁵

Aside from the impressive Deffufa, archaeologists have unearthed the Eastern Cemetery, which allows us to take a glimpse into Kerma's burial traditions. Located only a couple of miles to the east of the city, this cemetery was once the home to Kerma's rulers after they had passed to the afterlife. Since it functioned for nearly a thousand years, it is not surprising that the cemetery had over thirty thousand tombs. Some were covered with large mounds and encircled with cattle skulls; this perhaps signified the elite status of the deceased. Apart from kings and royals, these tombs also contain remains of human sacrifices along with other symbols of status, including jewelry and precious stones.

Kerma thrived under the careful supervision of their kings, who typically ruled with a mix of political cunning and military might. Although the full list of monarchs in Kerma is likely forever lost to us, some scholars agree that King Nedjeh was one of the most capable rulers of the kingdom. His reign (c. 1700 BCE) was often marked by interactions with none other than the neighboring Egyptians, but records suggest that the king was successful in taking over a few Egyptian forts in Nubia. His success inspired not only his own people but also some of the Egyptian soldiers who eventually chose to pledge their loyalty to him.

These two powerful forces usually alternated between peaceful trade, small skirmishes, and full-scale conflicts. There were times when the Egyptian pharaohs looked south to Kerma with admiration, but the majority of the time, the Egyptians were worried that Kerma would one day be unstoppable. Perhaps not planning on witnessing their nightmare turn into a reality, the Egyptians launched multiple incursions into Kerma, hoping they could curb their growth. However, Kerma's kings were steadfast in maintaining their autonomy. Their highly skilled archers and seasoned warriors allowed Kerma to always be ready to mount a defense. After all, by the time Egypt had turned its full focus southward, Kerma was no longer a mere trading post; it had already turned into an empire and was strong enough to put a halt to Egypt's expansionist ambitions.

That was until Pharaoh Thutmose I came to power sometime in the 16th century BCE. As the third pharaoh of the Eighteenth Egyptian Dynasty, Thutmose envisioned an Egyptian empire that stretched beyond the borders of the Nile Delta. In his eyes, Nubia—and Kerma by extension since it was the dominant force in the region—was an obstacle. Moreover, Kerma's gold deposits were so rich that the pharaoh thought it was a must for the Egyptians to secure the region.

Thutmose launched a major campaign in the second year of his reign. Armed with advanced weaponry and hardened by years of battle, the Egyptian forces marched southward, where they clashed with the mighty forces of Kerma. Although Kerma's elite archers and warriors seemed to succeed in repelling the attack, Thutmose's forces had no plans to back down. The Kerma warriors were gradually overwhelmed. Egyptian inscriptions and stelae recount that Thutmose himself participated in the war and successfully killed the Nubian king (most likely a reference to the king of Kerma). With Nubia brought under Egyptian control, Kerma's days as an independent power became a thing of the past.

Of course, the Egyptians did not stop with the fall of Kerma. To maintain control over the newly conquered region, the Egyptians installed an official known as the viceroy of Kush (also referred to as the King's Son of Kush) in the area north of the Third Cataract. This official served as a governor or the head administrator overseeing the former lands of Kerma and the entire Nubian region. Acting as Egypt's representative, the viceroy's responsibilities included ensuring order and loyalty to the Egyptian throne. Following the destruction of Kerma, the Egyptian pharaoh commissioned a new settlement just north of the former capital city. Named Dokki Geil (meaning "red mound"), this was the new power base for Egyptian rule in Nubia.

The Kingdom of Kush

Kerma's story ended with the Egyptian conquest, but this was not the end of Nubia. Around 1070 BCE, Egypt went through a major period of decline. Following the death of Pharaoh Ramesses XI in 1077 BCE, the Egyptians saw the departure of their golden age, known as the New Kingdom. From then on, Egypt's influence greatly weakened; the empire was suffering from division, losing power over distant regions, and struggling with both internal issues and outside invasions. However, it was during this turmoil (c. 1069 BCE) that a new power emerged from the remnants of Kerma: the Kingdom of Kush.

Taking advantage of Egypt's declining state as it entered the Third Intermediate Period, the Kushites worked to strengthen their hold. They chose Napata as their new capital, which was situated along the bank of the Nile and near the towering sandstone cliffs. From Napata, the Kushites were able to build their kingdom.

The first Kushite king, Alara, successfully united the Nubian territories under a single banner. Although there is not much information about him, it is safe to assume that his reign was prosperous. Alara was succeeded by Kashta, who was either his brother or son. Kashta was known to have great admiration for Egyptian culture. The very moment he was placed on the throne, the Kushite king wasted no time in "Egyptianizing" his kingdom.

However, his most significant move was when he placed his daughter, Amenirdis I, as the God's Wife of Amun at Thebes. Some claimed he was able to do so due to the positive relationship between the priests of Amun at Napata and those at Thebes. The position of God's Wife of Amun was first established during the Middle Kingdom. However, by the time Kashta rose to the throne, the position had grown so important that its political power was equivalent to that of the High Priest of Amun, who controlled Thebes. Through his daughter's high position, Kashta was able to establish a Kushite foothold within Egypt's religious hierarchy.

Meanwhile, the princes of Lower Egypt (northern Egypt) were too busy to notice this subtle assertion of power by the Kushites. They were embroiled in their own regional conflicts and power struggles, thus leaving the north politically divided and distracted. Seeing this as a golden chance, Kashta moved north into southern Egypt and declared himself king of Upper Egypt without initiating any kind of battle with the Egyptians. This laid the foundation of Egypt's Twenty-fifth Dynasty, better known as the Kushite dynasty.

Unfortunately, Kashta did not enjoy a long reign. Although records are scarce, it is likely that he ruled fewer than two decades before being succeeded by his son, Piye. Perhaps following in his father's footsteps, Piye continued to consolidate Kushite rule in the empire. With an army, Piye marched north, aiming to restore Egypt's traditions and unite the lands. In his eyes, this campaign was a holy war. Besides constantly offering sacrifices to the god Amun, Piye was also said to have commanded his men to ritually cleanse themselves before the beginning of each battle.

Despite succeeding in conquering all the cities of Lower Egypt, Piye never stripped the local rulers of their power. Instead, he allowed them to retain their positions and continued overseeing their lands as they had previously as long as they acknowledged him as their lord. Following the successful campaign in the Nile Delta, Piye sailed to Thebes and then returned to his homeland in Nubia. Interestingly, he never set foot in Egypt again and ruled the empire from afar.

Of course, the local kings of Egypt were free to rule as they wished, knowing that Piye was miles away from them. Rebellions soon took place, instigated by the royals of Lower Egypt. It was only when Piye's successor, Shabaka, rose to power that the Kushites were able to establish firm control over Lower Egypt all the way to the Nile Delta region.

Statues of Kushite rulers from the 7th century BCE.*

The Kushite pharaohs saw themselves as protectors of Egypt's sacred legacy. They believed it was their duty to uphold Ma'at, the Egyptian principle of cosmic balance. When Egypt saw the rise of another Kushite pharaoh, Taharqa, in 690 BCE, the empire witnessed a period of architectural grandeur and military achievements. Taharqa launched a number of monumental construction projects across Egypt and Nubia. The most significant of them was the completion of the Temple of Amun at Kawa in Nubia and the enhancement of the Temple of Karnak (one of the most important religious sites in Egypt) in Thebes.

Apart from his architectural projects, Taharqa also had his eyes on the battlefield. A few decades following his rise to the throne, Taharqa was left with no choice but to face the formidable Assyrian Empire under King Esarhaddon. The first campaign against the Kushite pharaoh was launched in 677 BCE, but Esarhaddon met with only limited success. A second mission was mounted in 674 BCE, but the Egyptians, under Taharqa, were able to repel the Assyrians.

Although Taharqa was able to keep Egypt safe from the Assyrians for a few years, he failed to stop the storm that was gathering on the horizon. Esarhaddon eventually succeeded in capturing Memphis in 671 BCE, prompting the Kushite pharaoh to flee south to Nubia. Taharqa planned to reclaim Egypt from the Assyrians, though his effort was in vain. His successor, Tantamani (who was also the son of Shabaka), continued to fight against the Assyrians, but under the leadership of Ashurbanipal, they proved to be unstoppable. This marked the end of Egypt's Kushite dynasty, as the Assyrians controlled Egypt in 666 BCE through a vassal king, Necho I. When Necho's son, Psamtik I, rose to power, the Egyptians freed themselves from Assyrian rule.

The ruins of Taharqa's pyramid.⁷

The Kushites soon faced attacks from the Egyptians under the command of Psamtik II. Kushite towns, monuments, stelae, and even temples were razed by the pharaoh, who was thirsty for a glorious military campaign. The Egyptians eventually got to Napata and destroyed the city before returning back to Egypt. Fortunately for the Kushites, they had already moved their capital farther south to the city of Meroë. This new capital was established sometime around 590 BCE. The Kingdom of Kush continued to bloom, and this shift to Meroë marked the beginning of the Meroitic period, a golden age in Kushite history.

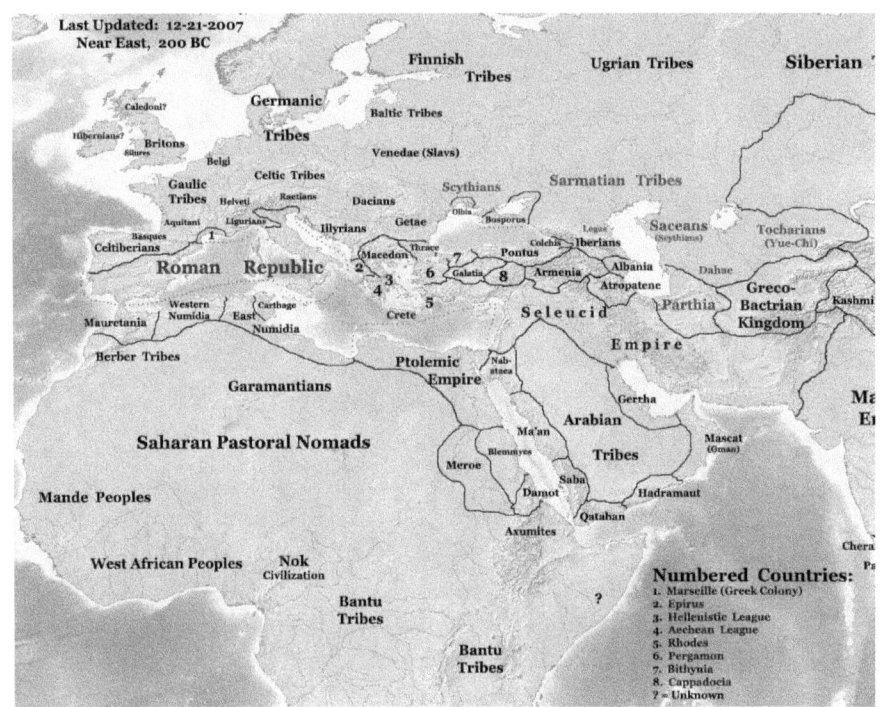

Map showing the city of Meroë and its surrounding neighbors c. 200 BCE.'

Since Meroë was located near vast iron deposits, the Kushites were able to develop a thriving iron industry, from weapons to various tools. Their skills working with iron were so renowned that traders from as far as Rome and China would flock to Meroë. Artisans were also the backbone of the city's economy. Their pottery, textiles, and fine jewelry, which blended both Kushite styles and Egyptian motifs, were highly sought after by various civilizations.

Meroë was the home to several Nubian pyramids; some of them (at least what is left of them) still stand today. While Egyptian pyramids were usually constructed as monumental structures with grand interiors, the Nubian pyramids at Meroë took on a more compact and steeply angled form. The Egyptian pyramids, such as the ones at Giza, took many years to be constructed. They featured several intricate inner chambers and passageways laden with treasures for the departed souls of their pharaohs. The pyramids in Meroë were less elaborate internally, as the Kushites preferred to focus more on building small chapels attached to the outside of each pyramid. These external chapels were where rituals could be performed, allowing the living to maintain a connection with the deceased.

The pyramids of Meroë.'

The new Kushite capital remained strong for years until the kingdom was brought into contact with a new formidable neighbor: Rome. With the fall of Cleopatra in 31 BCE and the incorporation of Egypt into Rome, Meroë lay directly on Rome's southern border. Tensions were on the horizon, which often resulted in conflicts with the Romans. The Kushite queen, Amanirenas, led her forces against the Romans around 25 BCE. Her surprise attack was a success; the Romans were caught off-guard and left with no choice but to witness their outpost turned into nothing more than just ruins.

Amanirenas was a force to be reckoned with. This was not her only feat; the Kushites also captured several Roman settlements, including the Egyptian city of Syene (modern-day Aswan). It was also under her leadership that the Kushites, perhaps portraying their defiance, managed to seize a bust of Emperor Augustus.

Skirmishes unsurprisingly continued between the two powers until a peace treaty was eventually agreed upon five years later. Through this, the Kushites were able to retain their independence and control over trade routes along the Nile. Rome agreed to withdraw to a position north of the First Cataract, thus establishing a stable frontier between the two powers.

Unfortunately for the Kushites, they saw the first few signs of their kingdom's decline by the 3rd century CE. Environmental degradation, possibly due to deforestation from the iron industry, proved to be one of the reasons behind their decline. The shifting trade routes also diminished the influence that Meroë once held. Political fragmentation might have also been one of the reasons behind Kush's ability to govern effectively. As time passed by, the once-bustling city began to show signs of decay.

The kingdom reached its final chapter when the Kushites witnessed the rise of the Kingdom of Axum (also spelled as Aksum) to the southeast. Scholars claim that Axumite forces invaded Kushite territory sometime in 330 CE, eventually marking the end of Meroë's reign. A stele near the ancient city cemented this claim even more. The artifact was attributed to an Axumite king, which suggests that the city might have fallen to foreign conquerors. This is only a theory, though, as there are others who argue that Meroë fell due to internal decline.

Chapter 2 – The Mysterious Land of Punt: Myths and Realities

The Story of the Rosetta Stone

Since the earliest days of human civilization, people have been driven by a desire to not only understand but also record the world around them, whether it is capturing their achievements, documenting their beliefs, or even communicating and connecting with the divine. When humankind progressed and began to develop more tools, they started to develop different ways of preserving their knowledge. Many civilizations invented methods for documenting history, each possessing its own unique features.

For example, the Sumerians in Mesopotamia invented cuneiform, the earliest form of writing. The cuneiform script was carved into clay tablets. In China, records were written on bones. This was known as oracle bone script and was typically used to predict future events and communicate with divine beings.

Of course, the forms of writing that we are familiar with today were preceded by these intricate systems that evolved over the centuries. More often than not, ancient languages were pictorial, which is where symbols are used rather than specific letters. These pictorial scripts often told stories in a visual language, much like how a picture can speak a thousand words.

Many agree that the most well-known and fascinating ancient writing system is Egyptian hieroglyphs. This form of writing was once etched onto temple walls, tombs, and scrolls. These carefully carved symbols once appeared vibrant with all their colors, but they were not merely for decoration. Hieroglyphs give us a window into the past, allowing us to take a glimpse into an ancient kingdom that existed thousands of years ago. The stories of a pharaoh's exploits, the Egyptians' religious rituals, and significant battles that took place along the Nile were immortalized in this script.

However, as time passed, these hieroglyphs turned into a mystery. Scholars across the world gazed at these symbols, but they could only wonder what they said. For a time, it appeared impossible to decipher the carvings and unlock the language of one of history's greatest civilizations.

Hieroglyphs carved onto a stele, now stored in the Louvre Museum.[10]

That all changed when a certain discovery shook the world in 1799. The story begins on a scorching summer day, the dust and sand of Egypt blowing in the air. Napoleon's army was near the town of Rashid, known by the French as Rosetta. They were stationed in this town while waiting for the next command for their campaign in North Africa. At the time, the soldiers were tasked with fortifying their defenses. Under the lead of Pierre-François Bouchard, a lieutenant and engineer of the French Army, they began working on rebuilding the crumbling fort near the city.

They dug through the debris, breaking apart centuries-old stones along the way. It was just a typical and mundane task that the military had to do during an invasion campaign, so they didn't think much of it—until one of their shovels struck something unusual. At first, Bouchard thought it was just another rock. Once they cleared away the dirt, the French lieutenant's eyes widened.

The French had discovered a large slab of stone built into a piece of wall. Bouchard brushed the dust away with his hand and immediately saw inscriptions carved onto the stone's gray granite-like surface. There were three distinct sections of text. At the bottom was an inscription in Greek, the middle section was in Demotic, and at the top were inscriptions written in hieroglyphs. Bouchard knew the finding was significant. The stone was transported to France, where it immediately sparked a wave of excitement among both intellectuals and linguists. This unexpected discovery was later named the Rosetta Stone, and scholars strongly believed that it held the key to understanding the ancient Egyptian script, a writing form that remained an intriguing mystery even for the brightest minds of that time.

One intellectual who became extremely enthralled by the discovery was Jean-François Champollion, a brilliant—some might also describe him as stubborn—linguist. Although Champollion was only a young man, he was thought to have possessed an insatiable curiosity and an exceptional gift for languages. The linguist had already mastered several ancient languages, including Latin, Greek, and Aramaic, but ancient Egyptian hieroglyphs remained an impenetrable wall.

The Rosetta Stone was not discovered in whole; a third of its top was broken. Champollion spent years studying the artifact. He faced skepticism from peers and intense competition from other scholars, yet the young linguist was confident that he would one day decipher the enigmatic text. His breakthrough came when he finally realized that the hieroglyphic text was not entirely symbolic as many had thought. The ancient writing was, in fact, a combination of phonetic and symbolic elements. By comparing the hieroglyphs to the Greek text, Champollion was able to slowly crack the code.

The Rosetta Stone, now displayed in the British Museum.[11]

He continued to work on the translation for several more years, and piece by piece, he successfully unlocked the meaning of each symbol. It was only in 1822—over two decades after the discovery of the Rosetta Stone—that Champollion was able to read the text that had been written thousands of years prior. Thanks to Champollion's translation, the ancient world of the pharaohs could be studied deeper. The hieroglyphs on scrolls, temple walls, and tombs were now readable.

Thousands of kings ruled ancient Egypt, and many of their lives (and even some of their names) are forever lost to time. However, these hieroglyphs brought to life the story of a few figures who left huge marks on the civilization. One of them was Pharaoh Hatshepsut, one of the few female pharaohs of Egypt. Ruling the land as a king (the symbols of kingship in Egypt were associated with masculinity), Hatshepsut left behind an account detailing a voyage to a land called Punt.

Often described as a land of riches, exotic goods, and divine offerings, the Land of Punt is a topic that has long fascinated historians. True, the hieroglyphs and accounts left by the pharaoh shed some light on this mysterious land, yet many questions remain unanswered. Where exactly was it located? What exactly was Punt? Was it a real place or only a myth used in Egypt's religious and political narratives?

The Egyptian Voyage to the Land of Plenty

The Land of Punt has been referred to by many other names, but according to ancient Egyptian texts, it was known as the Land of Plenty. Mentioned by the Egyptians as far back as the Old Kingdom (c. 2613-2181 BCE), the mysterious land was believed to be a significant trade partner with Egypt. Hatshepsut described the land with awe. Punt was more or less a paradise filled with an abundance of goods, all of which were highly prized in the kingdom along the Nile. The Egyptians often sailed to Punt to get their hands on gold, ivory, a myriad of exotic animals, myrrh, frankincense, and resin. Although these items were essential for the Egyptian economy, they were also commonly used in religious and spiritual rituals.

A relief of Egyptian soldiers during Hatshepsut's expedition to Punt.[12]

Frankincense was burned in temples; their prayers were believed to have been carried to the gods through the pleasant scent. The same could also be said of myrrh, but interestingly, resin was an important item in Egyptian burial practices. It was used to preserve bodies during the process of mummification.

On the walls of Hatshepsut's mortuary temple named Deir el-Bahri, Hatshepsut recorded not only the items that the Egyptians traded with Punt but also a description of the ambitious voyage to the mysterious land. The story started with the pharaoh commissioning a fleet of massive ships to travel across the Red Sea.

A voyage, no matter the size, was no small feat in the ancient world. The sea was very treacherous, and any journey was always fraught with danger. Back then, Egyptian ships were made of wood—primarily acacia and cedar imported from Lebanon—and bundles of papyrus reeds. They were powered by sails, and to navigate the waters, they required the strength and coordination of dozens of rowers.

Since this particular voyage was friendly, the Egyptians would have laden their ships with gifts and provisions for the people of Punt. By doing this, Hatshepsut was able to maintain not just a trade relationship with the Land of Plenty but also a diplomatic one.

The carvings that adorned Hatshepsut's mortuary temple captured the excitement and the importance of the voyage; it portrayed a sense of both adventure and divine purpose. In this ancient account, the pharaoh emphasized the journey's connection with the gods. She framed the expedition as a venture blessed by Amun, the chief god of the kingdom. The pharaoh believed that it was Amun's will that Egypt and Punt maintain a friendly relationship. By ensuring this, Hatshepsut would be showered with prosperity and divine favor throughout her reign.

Another relief from the Mortuary Temple of Hatshepsut depicting incense and myrrh trees obtained from Punt.[18]

After sailing the Red Sea, the Egyptians finally arrived at Punt, where they were said to have been greeted warmly by its inhabitants; this was illustrated on the reliefs. Interestingly, the hieroglyphs described the people of Punt as being rather distinct from the Egyptians. They dressed differently and had a different style of architecture. For instance, cone-shaped huts perched on stilts were common. Scholars thought this was possibly designed to protect against flooding or local wildlife. From the description of Punt's architecture alone, some scholars suggest that Punt's geography and climate were different from Egypt's, adding to the mystery of where the land might have been located.

In return for Punt's famous riches, the Egyptians traded their finely crafted goods. This ranged from tools to exquisite jewelry. Egypt also sent its most precious agricultural product: grains. Since Punt was clearly considered an equal in the eyes of the Egyptian pharaohs, gifts were said to have been presented with great reverence on both sides.

On the walls of Deir el-Bahri, one can also find striking depictions of trees from the Land of Punt, particularly the Boswellia tree, which was known for its fragrant resin. Hatshepsut might have ordered these trees to be uprooted and brought back to Egypt. Bringing live trees back across the desert was, of course, not a piece of cake. However, the Egyptians managed to do so. The Boswellia saplings were planted in the temple complex of Karnak. The trees symbolized wealth, religious devotion, and the success of Hatshepsut's reign.

Once the Egyptians returned to their homeland following the expedition, the treasures of Punt were paraded through the streets of Egypt. This was presumably done so that the pharaoh could make sure her people were aware of the journey's significance; it portrayed Hatshepsut as a leader capable of bringing divine favor to her kingdom. The incense and myrrh were burned in the temples of Egypt to honor gods like Amun, Osiris, and Hathor, with Hatshepsut's name linked to their acquisition.

Hatshepsut's expedition to Punt was one of the most remarkable episodes in the history of ancient Egypt. However, she was not the only pharaoh to have launched such a journey. Centuries before her reign, when Egypt was ruled by the Fifth Dynasty, one pharaoh had his focus on Punt. Known simply as Sahure, he ruled Egypt around 2450 BCE and is believed to have been one of the earliest known kings to have launched a successful expedition to the obscure yet prosperous land.

Under Sahure, Egypt witnessed a period of expansion and saw an increase in foreign trade. Like Hatshepsut, Sahure recognized the value that Punt held for both Egypt's economy and religious life. Based on surviving Egyptian texts and reliefs left by Sahure, scholars have learned that he sent fleets of ships southward across the Red Sea. While the exact harbor from which these ships departed remains uncertain, it is clear the Egyptians reached Punt and witnessed its precious resources firsthand.

Centuries later, during Egypt's Middle Kingdom period, the Red Sea harbor of Mersa Gawasis would emerge as a key launching point for similar expeditions to Punt. The Palermo Stone recorded in detail the treasure that the Egyptians obtained, though the unit they used is unspecified: 80,000 myrrh and malachite, another 6,000 electrum, and 23,020 staves made of ebony.

The Palermo Stone.[14]

While Hatshepsut ordered her people to bring back saplings of Boswellia, Sahure focused on bringing back exotic animals from Punt. His reliefs featured multiple ships returning to the Egyptian kingdom with an array of animals, from monkeys to leopards to other exotic creatures that were all prized for their rarity and religious importance. These animals were typically presented to the gods in various temples or kept in royal menageries where they were seen as embodiments of divine favor.

Although Sahure's expedition is considered less well known than that of Hatshepsut's, hieroglyphs give us insight into the importance of Punt even during the Old Kingdom. It provides concrete evidence that the relationship between these two lands was indeed long-standing; it endured across centuries and many dynasties.

The Main Question: Where Exactly is Punt Located on the Map?

Even though these Egyptian rulers left us with reliefs that depicted their expeditions to Punt, the exact location of the land remains one of the most intriguing mysteries of the ancient world. A number of scholars, historians, and archaeologists have tried to pinpoint the location of this fabled land, but for centuries, their efforts have led to only more questions and theories instead of answers. Since there were no surviving records from Punt itself, scholars are left with no choice but to rely solely on Egyptian texts and artwork to deduce the Land of Plenty's whereabouts.

Many theories have been made. One of the earliest came in the 19th century, which suggests that Punt could be located on the Arabian Peninsula, possibly in modern-day Yemen. Scholars back then arrived at this assumption based on the Egyptian texts that described how Punt was a land full of incense trees and spices. The geographical features of southern Arabia and the fact the region was known for its incense trade supported this theory. However, when further research was conducted with more advanced archaeological methods years later, scholars began to have second thoughts. It was also widely known that the Egyptians regularly traded with regions of Arabia, so it did not make sense for Hatshepsut to record the expedition in such an elaborate fashion. The reliefs of rhinoceroses, giraffes, and elephants also contradict the theory since none of these creatures were native to Arabia. Unable to find concrete evidence that could link Yemeni culture to Punt, most scholars have scratched this theory from their list.

The next theory claims that Punt was on a whole different continent. Instead of being somewhere in Asia, particularly on the Arabian Peninsula, Punt is thought to have been along the coast of the Horn of Africa, specifically in modern-day Somalia, Eritrea, or even possibly Djibouti. Scholars arrived at this theory based on the Egyptians' depictions of Punt's fertile landscape. It was a verdant land with myrrh trees and an array of exotic animals, including baboons and giraffes. These features are more closely associated with the Horn of Africa than the Arabian Peninsula.

The seafaring routes pictured in Egyptian hieroglyphs also indicate that Punt was reachable by sailing south across the Red Sea. It was believed that the Egyptians sailed down the Nile through the Wadi Tumilat (located in the Eastern Nile Delta). Here, they would disassemble their ships before carrying them overland toward the Red Sea. From here, they likely hugged the coastline, sailing south along the Red Sea, possibly reaching areas in what is now eastern Sudan, Eritrea, or northern Somalia. This coastal route supports the theory that Punt was located somewhere along the eastern African shore, though its exact location remains a subject of scholarly debate to this day.

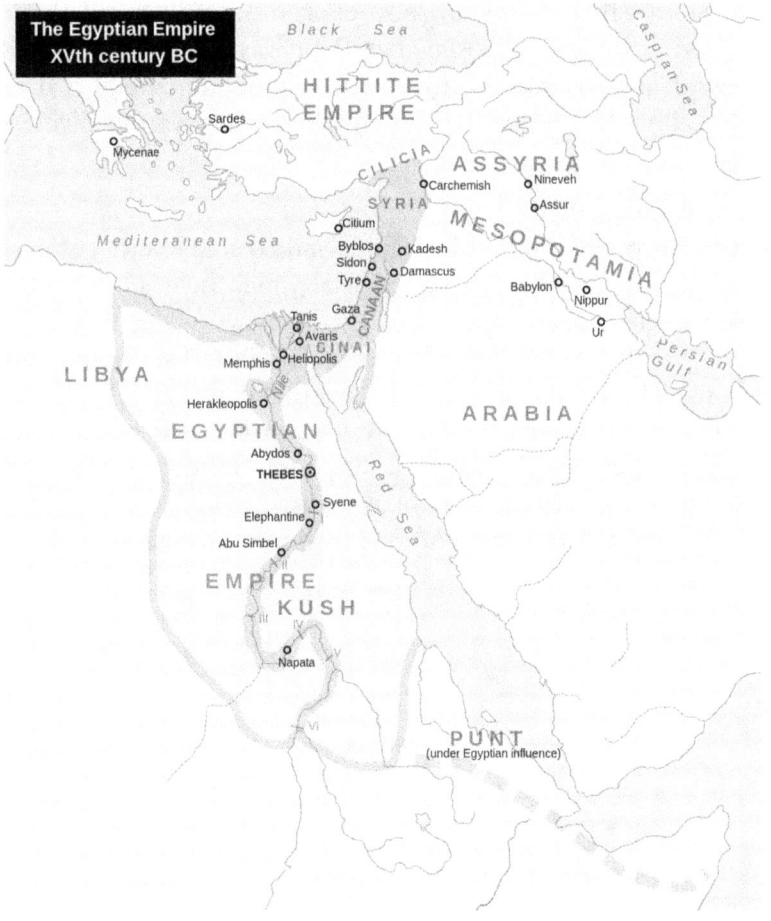

A map showing the commonly agreed location of Punt. [15]

Although this theory was first brought up in the 19th century, modern archaeologists still favor an East African location for Punt, with many strongly suggesting the modern-day Puntland of Somalia as the most likely candidate. Somalia had a long history of maritime trade and ancient connections with Egypt. It could very possibly be that the Land of Plenty once existed somewhere in this region. Additionally, Somalia's climate and biodiversity fit well with the Egyptians' description of the goods they brought back. The different species of exotic animals often depicted in the hieroglyphs of both Sahure and Hatshepsut also support the theory.

Regardless, no definitive evidence has been found to fully confirm the location of Punt. Despite the detailed account from the Egyptian records, they were not enough for the scholars to pinpoint a precise location. So, another theory arose to explain the mystery of Punt. This time around, scholars proposed that Punt was more of a symbolic or mythological land. It could have been an embodiment of a divine or spiritual realm where boundaries between Earth and the divine world blurred.

Punt as a Mythological Land

Ancient Egypt often infused religious and cosmic references into their historical record. According to ancient Egyptian beliefs, their pharaohs were not merely humans; they were also the shadows of the divine and appointed to be rulers by the gods themselves. Based on her inscriptions, Hatshepsut claimed to be the daughter of the goddess Hathor, who many thought to have resided in Punt. Since the Egyptians also believed that Punt was their ancestral homeland, it could be plausible that the depiction of Punt as a paradise-like land of abundance might have been an expression of Egypt's spiritual aspirations.

A relief at Deir el-Bahari depicting Hathor as a cow suckling the infant Hatshepsut.[16]

The idea of Punt as a divine land rather than a specific location on Earth is further supported by the reliefs at Hatshepsut's mortuary temple. These reliefs showed a distant country filled with goods and a place of almost supernatural beauty and abundance. The carvings of towering incense trees, exotic animals, and even beehives on stilts have led a few to believe that Punt was indeed a figment of imagination so the Egyptians could idealize the land of their gods.

This divine association is not surprising, considering how Egyptian cosmology placed significant emphasis on maintaining Ma'at, or the divine order of the universe. The pharaoh's expedition to Punt might have been about fulfilling a sacred duty to uphold this cosmic balance. Hatshepsut herself claimed through her reliefs that her expedition went beyond mere trade missions; it was said to be a sacred venture ordained by the gods, particularly Amun-Ra. By successfully returning to the kingdom with the riches of Punt, the pharaoh was ensuring that Egypt remained in harmony with the gods.

Despite direct expeditions to Punt becoming rarer over time (inscriptions detailing such expeditions became less frequent), Punt's religious and mythical significance persisted in Egypt's cultural memory. Centuries after Hatshepsut's reign, Punt was romanticized as an almost utopian land. It was seen as a distant paradise, and its exact location became less important than the idea it represented. Some may even agree that this idealization of Punt speaks to the broader human tendency to romanticize lost or unreachable lands.

This mythologizing of Punt probably grew when Egypt's power waned. With the rise of other civilizations, such as Rome, Egypt was no longer considered the only great civilization of the ancient world. So, the grand expeditions of pharaohs like Hatshepsut and Sahure were gradually forgotten, although the inscriptions remained on the temple walls. Eventually, Punt took on a mythical allure similar to that of the lost city of Atlantis. Although their exact locations have not been found, they continue to capture the imagination.

Nevertheless, mythical or real, it is clear that Punt once held immense importance for the ancient Egyptians. As modern technology and archaeological methods improve over time, there is hope that the mystery surrounding Punt will one day be solved and its precise location unveiled. Until archaeologists stumble upon that piece of evidence that could finally put all the debate to rest, for now, the Land of Punt will continue to remain in the chapter of lost worlds.

Chapter 3 – Nok and the Dawn of Ancient Nigeria

In ancient history, pottery and terracotta served as more than just functional items used for daily life. They were considered cultural markers and artistic achievements, but they were also thought to be a civilization's symbols of power. Through their distinguished techniques of shaping clay into vessels, figures, and statues, we can take a closer look into an ancient civilization's lifestyles, beliefs, and innovations.

One of the most awe-inspiring examples of terracotta in ancient history is the Terracotta Army of China, found in the tomb of Emperor Qin Shi Huang. Having been buried underground and covered by a large earth mound that resembled a natural hill, the burial complex was left untouched and survived the test of time. Believe it or not, it was discovered by local farmers in 1974. They had been digging a well during a drought. They found an immense collection of life-sized terracotta soldiers, chariots, and horses. These terracotta figures had been sculpted and left in the tomb to protect the emperor in the afterlife. Despite being over two thousand years old, the figures were pretty much intact. They had unique and different facial expressions and details in their armor. This find proved ancient China's incredible artistry and advanced pottery techniques.

The Terracotta Army.[17]

Of course, the Terracotta Army is not the only great example of the ancient world's abilities. The ancient Greeks displayed their own twist in making unique terracotta figures and pottery. They were often used in religious rituals, with the Greeks placing them in temples or graves as offerings to their gods. Meanwhile, in Mesoamerica, the Olmec civilization was famous for its terracotta heads and figurines that depicted its deities and rulers. These examples highlight the universal importance of pottery and terracotta in preserving the cultural and spiritual identities of many ancient civilizations.

Terracotta is known for its durability and malleability. Ancient artists often find it the perfect medium to express their creativity. Of course, as mentioned, these objects were not merely artistic expressions. Apart from its religious and spiritual purposes, they were also important for economic and domestic use. Thousands of years ago, pottery vessels played a vital role in trade and were typically used to store food, water, and other resources. In this sense, pottery served as a bridge between the mundane and the divine.

The Nok Civilization

In West Africa, this rich tradition of terracotta and pottery found a unique expression in the Nok civilization. Interestingly, this sophisticated civilization's existence was not known until 1928 when a small village known as Nok (located in the central highlands of Nigeria, about five hundred kilometers from Abuja) welcomed a group of miners. While searching for tin, these miners accidentally unearthed secrets that had been buried for centuries. The miners found a piece of terracotta. They were not aware of the significance of their find at first, but the co-owner of the mining partnership, Colonel Dent Young, sent the artifact to the Museum of the Department of Mines in Jos regardless.

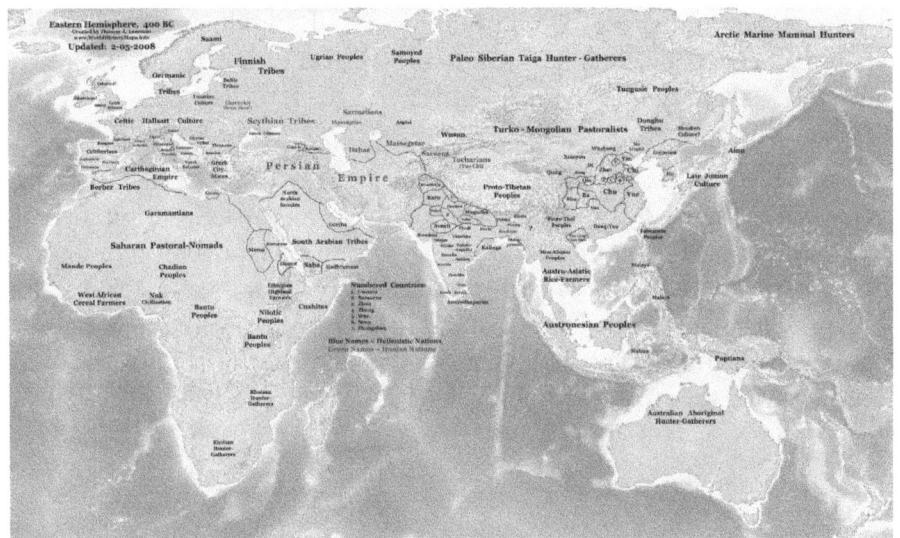

A map of the world c. 400 BCE.[18]

As mining activities continued in the regions of central Nigeria—including the Jos Plateau and the southern part of Kaduna—more artifacts were discovered. Several clay figurines were accidentally unearthed in 1943 near the village of Nok. One day, an unnamed clerk in charge of the mine discovered a rather strange terracotta head. Unaware that the head was an ancient artifact, he brought it back to his home. The head was placed in his yam field, where it acted as a scarecrow. This eventually caught the attention of Bernard Fagg, a British archaeologist and museum curator who was working as an administrative officer. Upon seeing the similarities between the terracotta head and the artifact discovered fifteen years prior, Fagg realized the world could be introduced to another ancient civilization that once thrived in the region.

After several excavations, archaeologists and scholars were finally able to reveal that the Nok civilization (named after the village where the artifacts were found) existed from around 1500 BCE to 200 CE. This was long before the rise of many West African kingdoms, such as the

Ghana Empire or the Mali Empire.

The most notable aspect of Nok culture was its terracotta figures, which were all expertly crafted. Pottery, in general, was undoubtedly a vital part of ancient life in many civilizations, yet the process of turning wet clay into bowls, plates, and especially more elaborate sculptures is not as simple as reciting one's ABCs. Once the clay was fired in an oven or kiln, gasses and vapors would build inside the hollow pottery. These expanding gasses eventually created pressure that led to cracks or, in some cases, shattered the pottery entirely.

However, potters developed a technique to prevent this from happening. They made vent holes in their pottery. These small openings gave way for the gasses to escape during the firing process. Nok artisans were masters of this method and did so with a certain level of creativity and artistry. Rather than creating random holes in the sculptures, the Nok people incorporated them subtly into the design of their figures. They turned these vent holes into a sculpture's eyes, nostrils, and mouths, giving their pieces a rather fluid and natural look.

A Nok sculpture, now on display at the Louvre.[19]

Although we do not know as much about the Nok civilization as we do about the ancient Roman, Greek, and even Chinese civilizations, many agree that Nok terracotta sculptures are easily recognizable for their unique style and artistry. Most of the time, their figurines were carved in a seated posture. Typically, they have one arm resting on a raised knee. As for the figurines' heads, they usually are large and elongated, with some taking up a significant portion of the sculpture's entire height. These figurines also had distinguishable facial features. Their eyes were hollow and carved in an almond shape, and their lips were usually parted. These features made the sculptures look otherworldly or even extraterrestrial-looking. Some of the male figures sport short, square beards and mustaches that grow at the corners of their mouths.

Of course, Nok sculptures were not only limited to human figurines. There are also beasts and creatures. The Nok were fond of sculptures that, to us, appear to be neither fully human nor purely animal. Despite having human bodies, these figures have animalistic features. Some have the head of a bird, complete with a beak and tail. There are others that have a combination of both human and animal features in the face; for example, it may have a human body with the head of an elephant that features human eyes and expressions.

These hybrid figurines suggest that the Nok people might have created these sculptures as representations of their spiritual or mythological beings. However, this is only speculation; the exact purpose of these terracotta figures is still a subject of debate. Since there are sculptures that have exaggerated physical conditions—such as those that seem to depict humans with elephantiasis or facial paralysis—certain scholars suggest they might have been used by the Nok as talismans to protect themselves against these ailments. Regardless of the real intentions behind these sculptures, it is clear that they were prominent in Nok culture.

Another fascinating discovery made by archaeologists through chemical analysis of the clay used in Nok pottery is that it all came from the same source. This finding led scholars to deduce that the production of pottery and terracotta figures might have been centralized and possibly controlled by a royal or an elite figure. If this was the case, then we can safely assume that the Nok had a highly organized society. The production of these goods would have been overseen to maintain a consistent quality and style.

A male figure from the Nok culture.[30]

The Nok Civilization's Advanced Metalworking

Believe it or not, the Nok civilization advanced straight from the Stone Age into the Iron Age, skipping the Bronze Age entirely. This significant transition sets them apart from many other ancient cultures. They eventually became known as one of the earliest known cultures in sub-Saharan Africa to perfect the iron-smelting technique—a technological advancement that greatly impacted their society. But, of course, the question remains: where exactly did this expertise in ironworking come from? Scholars have long debated this mystery, and to this day, there are three theories that suggest the origins of the Nok people's iron-smelting skills.

The first theory suggests that the knowledge came from the north, particularly the Phoenician city-state of Carthage in present-day Tunisia. As a major center of trade and culture in the ancient Mediterranean world, Carthage had established vast trade networks. As the empire expanded its influence through trade with sub-Saharan Africa, it could be possible that the knowledge of iron smelting was transmitted to the Nok civilization. However, there is not much evidence to confirm Carthage had this level of interaction with the Nok society. As of today, this theory remains nothing more than just a possibility.

The second theory points eastward, far into the land of Nubia, which was thriving along the Nile River (modern-day Sudan and southern Egypt). Nubia had a long history of metalworking, especially in copper and iron. It is possible that the Nok people's iron-smelting technology might have spread from Nubia through cultural and trade exchanges with East and West Africa. Although there is some archaeological evidence of Nubian ironworking predating that of the Nok, the lack of direct contact between the two regions makes it difficult for scholars to conclude Nubia's influence on the Nok people's iron-smelting skills. There are similarities in their techniques, yet that alone is not enough to fully support the theory.

Other scholars have arrived at the theory that ironworking in the Nok civilization was not brought by foreigners but was instead an invention they created on their own. It is plausible that the Nok people were the ones to have developed their iron-smelting techniques. This theory is further supported by the fact that there is no direct evidence of earlier metalworking cultures in the immediate vicinity of the Nok civilization. Perhaps the people discovered the process of smelting iron on their own after going through a series of experiments and out of necessity. If that were the case, then the Nok people could be named as the pioneers in sub-Saharan Africa. However, with limited archaeological records and the lack of written sources from the Nok themselves, it will be a long time before we can definitively prove the origins of their ironworking skills.

Due to the properties of iron (it is more durable compared to bronze) and its large quantities, the Nok were able to produce stronger tools and weapons. This gave them an advantage in agriculture, construction, and even warfare. Not only were they able to increase food production, but the Nok could also expand their territory greatly, eventually leading to the strengthening of their social and political structures.

One of the most important excavation sites that have given scholars a glimpse into the Nok's expertise in metalworking was Taruga. Located in the Abuja region of central Nigeria, excavations at this site revealed a total of thirteen furnaces along with a range of metal artifacts nearby. These furnaces were sophisticated for their time. They were designed to handle the high temperatures required to smelt iron. With materials like iron ore, charcoal, and copper alloys, the Nok craftsmen perfected techniques like casting, forging, and welding, all of which allowed them to produce items of various sizes and complexities.

These furnaces were crucial in the production of metal objects, from practical tools to weapons to decorative ornaments. Of course, the Nok people did not merely produce functional items that lacked creativity; they never failed to infuse their work with an artistic flair, demonstrating their eye for detail. Metal objects uncovered at Taruga, for example, were visually striking. They were usually decorated with intricate patterns, with geometric shapes and stylized animals being their most common motifs.

In the ancient world, iron was not merely a material for making tools and weapons. It was also a symbol of power. Clans or societies that had the most iron were seen as dominant forces in their regions. And so, with the ability to forge various iron weapons and tools, the Nok civilization was able to gain an edge over its neighbors. With stronger tools, they could farm more efficiently than others. They could clear more land for farming faster, expand their territories, and ensure a steady food supply. And with this flourishing agricultural activity, the Nok civilization would have experienced a growth in their population.

The Nok People and Their Beliefs in Curses

It is intriguing to consider the Nok people's religious and spiritual beliefs and how these might have influenced their societal structures. Despite not leaving us with written records that could detail their exact religious beliefs, scholars are confident that they practiced animism (the belief that natural elements like animals, trees, rivers, and even the smallest stones possess a spiritual essence), much like any other ancient civilization at the time.

One interesting aspect of their presumed belief system was the significant emphasis on the power of curses. The fear of invoking a curse—a spiritual retribution that could invite disaster upon a certain individual or even a family—likely played a vital role in maintaining the social order among the Nok people. This belief in the spiritual consequences of one's actions possibly suggests that they were deeply concerned with moral conduct and the harmonious functioning of society.

Direct evidence of the Nok judicial system is also unfortunately scarce, yet scholars suggest they might have established a few methods to address disputes and transgressions. It is plausible that minor civil cases, including but not limited to family disputes or false accusations, and more serious crimes, such as theft, murder, or adultery, were handled through communal gatherings. These gatherings were possibly held not only to solve disputes and punish the wrong but also to appease the spirits and restore balance within the community.

The Mystery Deepens

The mystery of the Nok civilization deepens with its sudden disappearance. So far, scholars have been unable to uncover any sort of archaeological evidence of the civilization after 200 CE. The reason behind this has long puzzled scholars. Although no definitive answer has been confirmed, a few possible theories have been put forward to explain the mystery.

One of the theories suggests that the Nok people might have faced rapid decline due to the overexploitation of their natural resources, especially since the people relied heavily on charcoal for iron smelting. If they constantly worked the furnaces, the Nok people would have needed large quantities of charcoal. This possibly led to deforestation, depleting the land's ability to support agriculture. If that were the case, society would have become vulnerable to collapse. Forests disappearing faster than one could imagine, poor soil quality, and declining food production would lead to famine. It would not be surprising if we one day learn that this was, in fact, the factors that contributed to the decline of their population.

Other scholars believe it was climate change. Gradual shifts in weather patterns, including prolonged droughts or even changes in rainfall, might have disrupted the delicate balance of Nok agriculture. If the Nok people were heavily reliant on their crops, any environmental shift could have had devastating effects. It is also plausible that their population dwindled due to diseases that were unfamiliar to them. Back then, diseases could easily spread unchecked. And without modern medical knowledge, a pandemic or epidemic could wipe out a massive part of a population. Fierce invasions from neighboring groups of people could have also contributed to the Nok people's decline; with their settlements overrun, survivors might have had no other choice but to flee or perhaps integrate into another culture.

Regardless of the exact factors behind their disappearance, the Nok civilization did leave a lasting legacy on the cultures that followed them. In fact, their influence can be seen today, especially in the artistic traditions and technological advancements of later Nigerian civilizations. The Ife civilization, which began flourishing in the 11th century CE, might have gained inspiration from the iron and terracotta works crafted by the Nok people.

The culture of another wealthy society in southeastern Nigeria, the Igbo-Ukwu, also bore a slight resemblance to that of the Nok civilization. Thriving around the 9th century CE, the Igbo-Ukwu were best known for their advanced metalworking and sophisticated bronze artifacts. The Igbo-Ukwu bronze bowl, complete with a twisted rope design and detailed geometric patterns, appeared to have been made through advanced casting techniques that paralleled the skill of Nok artisans.

Similarly, the fly-whisk handle discovered at Igbo-Ukwu (the name of a site) might also have roots in the Nok people's early sculptural traditions. Shaped like a human figure with detailed facial features and body adornments, the discovery of this artifact reveals a shared heritage of metalworking expertise and aesthetics that aligns with the foundations laid by the Nok people centuries before. Of course, precise links between these civilizations remain speculative. Yet, as for now, it is safe to assume that the Nok people's achievements in iron smelting and artistry did lay the early foundations for the technological and cultural advancements of later West African civilizations.

Chapter 4 – The San and the Early Tribes of Africa

The sun had just risen, shining its first rays over the dry savannah. Far in the distance was a small group of hunters, each crouched low in the bush. One of them, perhaps the leader of the group, had his eyes locked on a small herd of antelope grazing in the distance. Believe it or not, these hunters had been tracking these creatures since dawn. They had been following the faintest tracks left in the ground by the antelopes' hooves. Suddenly, a slight breeze blew. Quickly but patiently, he grabbed a handful of dust and threw it in the air—this was a way to test wind direction. Confident that the wind was on their side—the dust blew away from the herd—the hunter signaled the rest to move in closer.

Of course, hunting game was not supposed to be rushed. Their movements were slow, deliberate, and cautious. They did not want to alert their prey. These hunters had a small bush in one of their hands, which they used to camouflage themselves with the landscape as they crawled across the open ground. They held a bow in the other.

The hunters knew the habits of these animals well, from the way they moved to the location where they drank water from and even how they rested. All those years of experience had taught these hunters to easily read the land and all the creatures that inhabited it.

San hunter preparing a poison arrow.[21]

As they moved nearer, the hunters slowly selected a reed arrow from their quiver, which was slung over their backs. These arrows, however, were not the usual ones used in wars. The tip of the arrow was smeared with a certain deadly poison made from the larvae of a small beetle. Sometimes, the hunters used venoms that they had extracted from various plants and even venomous snakes. For bigger and tougher game, the hunters used a poison that they extracted from a type of caterpillar they called *ka* or *ngwa*.

This small reddish-yellow caterpillar often grows up to three-quarters of an inch long. To make the poison, the hunters typically boiled the caterpillars a few times until the liquid turned into a red jelly. After a period of cooling, the hunters applied the poison to their arrows. They never applied it on the tip; instead, they applied it just slightly below the tip so that the poison was safely contained within a reed collar to prevent accidental injuries. Once the arrow pierced its target, the poison would gradually take effect, attacking the animal's nervous system and eventually rendering it paralyzed.

However, despite the lethal nature of the poison, it did not contaminate the entire animal. Only the part where the arrow pierced through was cut out and thrown away. The rest of the meat was cooked and consumed.

As for our hunters, they lay low, waiting for the right moment. Once an antelope moved into range, one of the hunters raised his bow and, with practiced precision, released the arrow. The shot landed in the antelope's side. The creatures bolted and, in a few seconds, disappeared into the bushes. The hunters did not follow right away; they knew it would be hours before the poison did its work.

While they waited, the hunters checked the traps they had laid in different spots across the hunting ground. Some were empty, while a few others had hares and guinea fowls. Once they collected these smaller animals from the traps, the hunters moved on, tracking the wounded antelope. They looked for any sign of the antelope's path, such as broken twigs or the occasional drop of blood along the dry ground.

The sun was high, and the hunters were beginning to feel thirsty after hours of traveling under the scorching heat. A few of them drank from an ostrich eggshell that they had filled with water, while others dug holes in the sand to find water. Finally, the hunters found their antelope. It was lying on the ground, its energy drained by the slow-acting poison. The leader of the hunters approached the creature carefully, showing respect for the life that had been taken. To them, these hunts provided more than just food; it was also a connection to the land and the ancient ways of their people.

These hunters were a part of the San, one of the oldest inhabitants of southern Africa (particularly in the vast, rugged landscapes that stretched across modern-day Botswana, Namibia, South Africa, and parts of Angola and Zimbabwe). The San lived as nomadic hunter-gatherers for thousands of years. Their connection to the land and their exceptional mastery of survival made it possible for them to find sustenance where others might only see wilderness. Living on the dry lands for thousands of years, it is not surprising that the San developed a culture built around cooperation and respect for the natural world. They possessed a deep understanding of the flora and fauna that shared their land.

Meanwhile, our hunters safely returned to their camp. Here, they shared the kill with the tribe, as was their custom. Typically, the meat would be roasted over a fire. Since the San were not wasteful people, they would use every part of the animal. The hide, for instance, would be tanned and turned into a blanket, while the bones would often be cracked for the marrow. Each part of the animal had its own purpose, and the parts were seen as gifts from the earth that sustained them.

The Culture and Beliefs of the San People

Interestingly, the San people had no formal chiefs or any sort of centralized authority figures. Instead, they functioned through group consensus. Whenever there was a dispute brewing among them, the involved parties would typically gather for lengthy discussions. Each of them was given a chance to voice their opinions. This would go on until a resolution was reached.

Unlike many other groups of people across the world, leadership for the San people was not inherited but rather granted based on their expertise in specific areas, such as hunting or the spiritual realm. This governance structure often baffled many, especially the European colonists later on. Europeans often had trouble negotiating treaties with the San since there was no central leader among them.

Another interesting aspect of the San people's leadership was that it was always shared. The tribe valued equality, especially when it came to essential resources and supplies. Meat gathered from hunts and traps was distributed not only to their group members but also to the entire tribe. By doing this, the San were able to strengthen their social bonds and ensure collective survival at all times. Even visitors were invited to eat with the San. However, this was done with the expectation that their generosity would be reciprocated by their visitors in the future.

While men played large roles in the tribe's survival, women had their own responsibilities. They spent their day gathering edible plants, such as mushrooms and berries. Since these women, like their male counterparts, had deep knowledge of their surroundings, they were able to forage for food even in the harshest of conditions. These plants, however, were not shared with the entire tribe but consumed only by immediate family members. Apart from gathering food, San women were also responsible for nursing children. They brought their children with them wherever they went, including when they were out gathering resources.

Perhaps the most distinguishing feature of the San people was their ancient rock art, which provide us with a window into their world. This art, typically found in caves and rock shelters, is scattered throughout southern Africa and is among the oldest known forms of art in human history. Striking images of the San hunting, dancing, and performing different kinds of rituals were all painted with natural pigments.

Rock paintings by the San found near Murewa, Zimbabwe. [23]

Just like many other civilizations and tribes in the ancient world, the San belief system was both rich and complex. It revolved around the worship of a supreme god, other minor deities, and the spirits of ancestors. One of the most significant spiritual beings often mentioned in their mythology is known as |Kaggen (sometimes spelled as Cagn). Described to be a trickster deity, |Kaggen could transform into a number of animals, with the most common ones being an eland (a kind of antelope), a praying mantis, a snake, and a vulture. Although the deity was thought to be mischievous, |Kaggen was also regarded by the San as a creator figure. |Kaggen was the god responsible for shaping the world.

The eland was thought to have played a central role in the religious beliefs of the San people. Depictions of this creature can often be seen in their rock art. The eland is a species of antelope native to southern Africa and is best known for its imposing size and grace. It can grow up to five feet tall. Male elands can weigh up to almost two thousand pounds. Apart from its muscular build, an eland also sports spiral horns that curve elegantly outward. While it is common to spot an adult eland with a light brown or tan coat with faint white stripes along its side, the older males usually have a rather bluish-gray hue. Although the creature is considered big, elands are agile; they can easily leap over obstacles.

A common eland, typically found in eastern and southern Africa.[28]

The San people held this creature in high regard, seeing it as a symbol of strength and fertility. Thus, it is not unusual that the antelope was involved in a number of the San people's rituals. The four key rituals featuring the eland were a boy's first kill, a girl's puberty rites, marriage ceremonies, and trance dances. As for boys, successfully killing an eland marked their passage into adulthood. Its fat would then be extracted and used in the ritual feasts. During a girl's puberty ritual, women would perform the eland bull dance, which mimicked the antelope's mating behavior. This ritual was believed to have been done to ensure the girl's beauty, health, and good fortune.

Whenever the San suffered from sickness or disease, they would perform a certain ritual dance that they believed could heal the group. Sometimes referred to as the healing dance, this ritual was held by shamans, but everyone in the tribe participated. The ritual began with women sitting around the central fire as they sang and clapped their hands. The men would then dance around the women in a clockwise direction and then anti-clockwise. As the rhythms intensified, the dancers would reach a state of unconsciousness or a trance, where it was believed that their souls were transported to the realm of the spirits.

Here, they could plead with the spirit to heal the sickness that plagued their group.

The San were able to preserve their rich customs and traditions through their rock art and oral traditions. They told stories of their gods and ancestors, moral lessons, and their knowledge of nature, which were useful for future generations. Even as they faced changing times, their spiritual connection to the land, their respect for nature, and their communal way of life continued to define their identity.

The Khoikhoi, Southern Africa's Early Pastoralists

One of the earliest pastoralists who made the plains of southern Africa their home was known as the Khoikhoi. Some may know them by the name "Hottentots," a term used by early European settlers. However, "Hottentot" is now recognized as a colonial and derogatory label. It was used by the early Europeans based on how they perceived the Khoikhoi language, particularly the distinctive click sounds, which they found unfamiliar and mocked. Over time, the term became associated with stereotypes and was used in a dismissive, dehumanizing way. Today, the proper and respectful name is "Khoikhoi," which means "real people" in their language.

This group of people was absolutely distinct from the San in both lifestyle and societal structure. While the San lived as hunter-gatherers, the Khoikhoi embraced a pastoral way of life. They raised livestock and had highly innovative herding techniques. They were able to thrive in even the harshest landscapes of southwestern Africa. They rotated grazing lands to prevent overgrazing and knew about the water sources in their territories. It is safe to say that their society, which existed for thousands of years, has left a lasting legacy on the region, even when European contact later transformed their world.

Based on archaeological findings, the Khoikhoi had been surviving in the southwestern part of Africa since 2000 BCE. Since they were semi-nomadic, the Khoikhoi moved with the seasons. They often followed water sources and searched for suitable grazing lands for their herds of cattle and sheep. Of course, given their nomadic lifestyle, their settlements were rather simple, marked by circular huts made from woven reeds and branches. These structures could easily be dismantled, making it possible for them to travel across the vast landscapes of southern Africa in places like modern-day Namibia and Botswana.

A depiction of the Khoikhoi dismantling their huts and getting ready to move to another location.[24]

The Khoikhoi also had a rather organized structure. They were often organized into clans or family groups. Each of these clans was led by a chief. While the original Khoikhoi word for their chief is not well documented, European settlers referred to these leaders simply as "captains." Along with a council of elders, the captain would be the one responsible for making decisions, from handling disputes to deciding where to move next.

These people valued autonomy, but like the San, they worked together, especially when facing obstacles and difficulties. Whenever their land was terrorized by famine or drought, the Khoikhoi would work to save their clans. This social organization allowed them to maintain a sense of not only unity but also resilience in a changing environment.

The Khoikhoi relied heavily on animal husbandry and viewed their cattle as more than just a source of food. Besides providing them with milk, meat, and hides, cattle were also considered a symbol of wealth and status. The more livestock a Khoikhoi clan or family owned, the more powerful they became.

Like the San, the Khoikhoi left us with rock art. Cave walls and shelters were decorated with drawings that depicted their daily lives, animals, and spiritual beliefs. Though they were not as detailed as San rock art (the San painted with brushes, while the Khoikhoi only used their fingers), the Khoikhoi paintings have provided us with insights into their culture.

Their relationship with the San was rather complex. There were times when the two groups were cooperative, but at some point, tensions led to arguments. Despite the two groups of people sharing the same land for millennia, they did not always see eye to eye due to their differences in lifestyle. The Khoikhoi's more hierarchical and structured society differed greatly from the San people's egalitarian way of life. While the Khoikhoi traded livestock with the San in exchange for other goods, competition for resources often led to friction between the two.

In the 17th century, the Khoikhoi saw their way of life change. It began when the Dutch first landed on the Cape of Good Hope in 1652. They were met by the Khoikhoi, whose vast lands and thriving livestock attracted the attention of these foreigners. The Khoikhoi engaged in trade with the Europeans, but peace was not meant to last long.

As the Dutch settlers' demand for land and livestock grew, the Khoikhoi were eventually pushed off their ancestral lands by the foreigners. Their herds were greatly diminished. As the settlers claimed more land for farming, the Khoikhoi people's traditional semi-nomadic lifestyle became untenable. Some were even forced to labor for the Europeans, losing their independence in just the blink of an eye.

The Khoikhoi suffered a smallpox epidemic in the 18th century, which further devastated their population. Countless clans were wiped out, leaving their society in ruins. What had once been a thriving pastoralist culture now struggled to survive, their traditional way of life a thing of the past.

Yet, the Khoikhoi people did not vanish entirely. Their descendants live on today, particularly in Namibia and South Africa, where their cultural legacy is being revived through language, art, and heritage movements.

The Nguni Peoples

Southern Africa was also the home of the Nguni people. Their roots trace back to around 500 CE. The Nguni are considered to be one of the largest ethnic groups in the region; the Bantu-speaking Nguni have gradually spread across what is now South Africa, Eswatini, and southern Mozambique. The early Nguni communities, which included the Xhosa, Zulu, and Swazi, were known for their complex social structures and pastoral lifestyles.

Like the Khoikhoi, the Nguni were primarily pastoralists. They typically raised cattle, which also played an important role in their society, both economically and spiritually. Since cattle were symbols of wealth and status, herds were used by the Nguni to measure a family's reputation and prosperity. They also practiced agriculture, although it was limited. Millet and sorghum were common crops planted by them, and they complemented their cattle herding. However, since the Nguni had a pastoral lifestyle, they were semi-nomadic, often moving from one location to another to find better grazing lands.

The social organization of the Nguni was built around a clan-based system. These clans were led by a chief whom they referred to as the inkosi. Besides maintaining order, the inkosi was in charge of overseeing the welfare of the community—much like the responsibilities of every other leader of a clan. Within each clan, family groups were structured around kinship ties, with land and resources being inherited through both the mother's and father's lines.

Interestingly, each Nguni tribe developed its own cultural practices and identity that are distinct from each other. The Xhosa, for one, were among the first Nguni groups to migrate southward, settling in the fertile regions of the Eastern Cape. They also had a complex hierarchical society where leadership was passed down through hereditary chiefs. Given their proximity and interaction with the San people, the Nguni language was known for its "click" sounds, which were common among the San.

A depiction of the Xhosa painted by the English artist and explorer Thomas Baines. [25]

The Xhosa were known to have practiced a form of marriage arrangement called ukuthwala. This traditional practice, also known as bride kidnapping, sparked controversy over time; today, most nations would consider it a sex crime. Men were allowed to abduct a woman of their choice and force them into marriage without the consent of their parents. There were also cases where men resorted to paying the father—or legal guardian—of the woman they desired with cattle in exchange for her hand in marriage. The practice of ukuthwala also allowed for a different scenario, one that involved lovers who wished to be together but whose union was opposed by their families.

Of course, despite being a long-standing tradition in Xhosa society and several other tribes in the region, ukuthwala has become extremely controversial in modern times. The practice was often abused and led to young women being taken against their will, usually by much older men.

The broader Nguni society also included the Zulu. The Zulu started off as nothing more than a small clan and eventually established themselves in the eastern regions of present-day South Africa. Similar to other Nguni groups, the Zulu were organized around kinship and clan systems. Their clan leaders were known as amakhosi, and they held considerable influence over social and political matters within their communities. While they were traditionally grain farmers, the Zulu also took care of large herds of cattle. When it was time for them to replenish their herds, the Zulu would sometimes launch raids on their neighbors and seize their cattle.

Last but not least, there is the Swazi. The Swazi were also pastoralists, and they mainly settled in the mountainous regions of what is now Eswatini. Their society was organized under a dual monarchy. The governance was shared between a king (Ngwenyama) and a queen mother (Ndlovukati). The Swazi are best known today for their rich cultural heritage, from their intricate beadwork to ritualistic dances to oral traditions. Their most well-known tradition is the Umhlanga (Reed Dance) ceremony, which is celebrated annually as a tribute to unity, cultural pride, and community bonds.

More often than not, the early Nguni peoples had interactions with neighboring groups, such as the San and the Khoikhoi. Through these interactions, the Nguni were able to harness their hunting skills and various foraging techniques. In exchange, the Nguni shared their expertise in cattle herding with them. The Nguni also engaged in trade with Bantu-speaking communities farther north, with cattle and agricultural products being exchanged for precious goods, including iron and pottery.

By the end of the first millennium, the Nguni people had successfully established strong and organized societies across southern Africa. Their settlements, rich cultural traditions, and development laid the foundation for the social and political structures that would shape southern Africa long before the arrival of European colonists.

Chapter 5 – Carthage beyond Hannibal

A princess sailed across the seas. However, this was not an ordinary royal voyage. Dido, a princess from Phoenicia, was actually fleeing from tyranny. The daughter of the wealthy king of Tyre (modern-day Lebanon), Dido never thought this day would come, but her world had been shattered by the treachery of her own brother, Pygmalion. After seizing the throne following their father's death, Pygmalion murdered Dido's beloved husband, hoping to secure his power. Faced with the cruel reality of her own brother's rule, Dido decided to leave the only home she had ever known. After gathering those loyal to her, the princess set out on a journey, their destination uncertain.

Their voyage across the Mediterranean was, of course, long and fraught with peril. However, Dido and her followers eventually found land. They arrived in North Africa, where the land was controlled by the Berber tribes. Legend has it that the Berber chieftain, upon witnessing the foreigners disembark, was wary of them, thinking they were there to bring war and bloodshed. But Dido came in peace and requested nothing but some land for her people to settle. The chieftain hesitated at first but later agreed to Dido's request with one condition. The Phoenician princess could take as much land as an ox hide could cover.

The Berber chieftain thought Dido would only obtain a small and inconsequential piece of land. However, he had underestimated her. Instead of laying a single piece of ox hide on the ground, Dido cut it into thin strips. She then laid them end to end in a circle around a high hill, later known as the Byrsa. With her cunning, she was able to claim the entire hill for her people. It was a strategic spot; the hill overlooked the sea and seemed perfect for a brand-new city. This was the legendary foundation of the city of Carthage.

The ruins of Carthage.[36]

The ancient poet Virgil said Dido was an impressive and resourceful queen. In his epic *Aeneid*, the poet claimed that she built the city from the ground up, transforming it from a simple settlement on a hill into a thriving metropolis. Under Dido's watchful eye, Carthage's reputation skyrocketed, attracting traders and settlers from lands far away.

However, whether or not this legendary account holds any truth has been debated by scholars and historians for centuries. Some even question Dido's very existence. Still, the traditional founding of Carthage in 814 BCE fits with what we know from archaeology, which suggests the story might hold a kernel of truth.

Historical facts suggest that the city started as a modest port where Phoenician traders often stopped to resupply, repair their ships, and trade. Due to the strategic location of Carthage, it became a must-stop for the Phoenician traders who sailed between their homeland and the far reaches of the Mediterranean. At the time, the city was known as one of many Phoenician settlements scattered along the coasts of North Africa and the Mediterranean islands, and it remained this way for years. Changes only came in 332 BCE when Alexander the Great besieged and eventually destroyed the great city of Tyre.

For a long time, Tyre had been a bustling hub of trade and industry. It was a center of wealth for the Phoenician world. Its destruction sent shockwaves across the Mediterranean. Many of its wealthiest citizens managed to flee before Alexander's army could breach Tyre's walls. These people were either wealthy merchants, industrialists, or elites who had enough resources to buy their freedom from Alexander's advancing troops. With their coffers still full of gold, these people—or rather refugees—left Tyre to seek a new home, which they eventually found in Carthage.

The influx of these Tyrians, who brought along not only their wealth but also their knowledge and expertise in trade, shipbuilding, and various other industries, almost immediately transformed Carthage from a mere port into a flourishing economic powerhouse. Within years, Carthage's reputation had eclipsed Tyre, becoming the new nucleus of Phoenician trade in the Mediterranean. Its location on the North African coast meant it was at the crossroads of the western Mediterranean and the Levant. Carthage was able to control commerce between the eastern and western Mediterranean with ease, allowing the city to rise as a dominant force in the region.

The Wealthy City

Carthage's immense wealth came neither entirely from its military might nor its advantageous geography. Despite being well known for its rivalry with Rome and its involvement in the Punic Wars, the story of Carthage is more than just wars and violence. Before the chaotic episodes of war, Carthage had been one of the richest cities in the ancient world.

A bustling metropolis, the city had distinct residential areas. The citadel was perched atop the Byrsa, and the hill was surrounded by four main residential sections. The city's formidable walls stretched at least twenty-three miles, providing Carthage with defense.

Of course, like many other major ancient cities, Carthage had all the trappings of urban sophistication. There were theaters so the population could enjoy entertainment, a myriad of temples for religious observances, and a necropolis for the dead to rest in peace. However, being a city of trade and agriculture, Carthage's symbol of economic and naval power was the Great Harbor.

An illustration of Carthage. The circular harbor at the front is the Cothon.⁷

Although this type of artificial water reservoir was common in Phoenician-controlled lands, including Sicily and Cyprus, the one in Carthage was particularly renowned due to its impressive size and design. It had two different sections. The outer harbor was for commercial purposes. Rectangular in shape, this harbor was often filled with hundreds of trading ships from all over the Mediterranean. The harbor was also surrounded by tall, grand structures complete with columns and arches that made the busy commercial district appear elegant. There were workshops and warehouses in which oars, rigging, wood, and canvas were stored. This made it easy for merchants to load and unload their cargo and repair their ships.

The commercial harbor was connected directly to the second and inner section of the Grand Harbor. This circular military harbor—referred to as the Cothon by the ancient Greeks—was equally impressive, but just as its name suggests, it served an entirely different purpose. The harbor had about 220 covered docks, where Carthaginian warships or quinqueremes were stored, and slipways, allowing for quick deployment when needed.

Interestingly, at the center of the Great Harbor stood a small island where the naval command center was located. This was where the admiral oversaw the entire harbor and the sea. Whenever a threat could be seen in the distance, the main entrance of the Great Harbor would be blocked by iron chains.

Metals like gold, silver, tin, copper, and iron flowed through the city, as did other popular goods, such as animal hides, wool, amber, ivory, and incense. Slaves were also commonly traded in Carthage's markets. The city boasted an array of workshops that produced beautiful and highly sought-after goods, especially for the elites. This included finely embroidered textiles, luxurious carpets, and the famous purple-dyed cloth that came from the Murex shellfish (the same purple worn by Roman emperors and elites).

Perhaps following in the footsteps of their Phoenician ancestors, Carthaginian traders were experts in moving goods across the sea. They could sell anything with just about anyone and always made a profit. According to one story recorded by the Greek historian Herodotus, the Carthaginians ventured beyond the Pillars of Hercules (referred to as the Strait of Gibraltar today) and sailed along the North African coast to trade with indigenous peoples who inhabited the remote areas. Once they arrived, the Carthaginian traders unloaded their goods and signaled the local inhabitants by lighting a smoky fire. These traders would then retreat to their ships.

Seeing the clouds of smoke in the air, the locals would come to the beach and take a look at the Carthaginians' goods. They would then place gold next to the goods they wished to trade and left. The Carthaginians returned to check the gold; if they were satisfied with the amount of gold offered, they would take it and leave. If not, the traders would wait until more gold was added. Only when both sides were satisfied would the trade be complete. According to Herodotus, neither side ever tried to cheat the other, which is impressive.

These lands along the North African coast were not the only places where the Carthaginian traders flocked; their trade network stretched far into the bustling markets of Athens, Delos, and Syracuse, where they even had their own permanent quarters. Modern archaeologists uncovered Punic amphorae (a type of pottery vessel used by the Carthaginian traders to store and transport goods like wine, olive oil, and garum) in various locations as far away as Marseille, Corsica, and Rome, which further proved the city's wide-reaching trade network.

A silver Carthaginian coin.[38]

Of course, Carthage did not only send its goods out into the world; the city also welcomed traders from other kingdoms and empires as well. Merchants from Rhodes, Athens, and the Italian Peninsula were common in Carthage. They were all treated with the same respect as local merchants, which made Carthage a safe hub for commerce. The city also introduced Carthaginian coinage in the 5th century BCE, and the Ptolemies of Egypt adopted the same Phoenician coin standard. Transactions between the two of them became smoother.

It is hard to dismiss that trade was the lifeblood of Carthage. However, the city also thrived in another venture: agriculture. Carthage had fertile lands, and the Carthaginians made the most of them. Gardens filled with grapevines, olive trees, and vegetables and fields of grain were common sights in the areas surrounding Carthage. They were fed by small irrigation canals. The Carthaginian farmers cultivated their land with impressive efficiency. Their produce was then sold in local markets or shipped across the seas, adding to the city's coffers.

The famous ancient agricultural writer Mago was from Carthage. Although his original Punic text, which was divided into twenty-eight volumes, has been lost, parts of the Greek and Latin translations survived the test of time, giving us a peek into ancient Carthage's farming techniques. Mago wrote about crop rotation, proper plowing depths, manure use, selecting healthy livestock, vine grafting, and even beekeeping.

While Carthage continued to thrive, their wealth and prosperity soon made the city a target. In 310 BCE, the city saw a threat brewing in the distance when Agathocles of Syracuse launched an invasion of North Africa. Seeing Carthage's richness as a way to fund his upcoming military campaigns, Agathocles sought to conquer the city. He achieved success in the beginning stage of his conquest mission; however, the Carthaginians eventually managed to turn the tide. With the support of the local Libyan and Berber populations, who sided with Carthage without hesitation as a result of the city's fair treatment, Agathocles was driven out of North Africa.

As the city's wealth and power continued to grow, expansion became inevitable. The Carthaginians began to establish more colonies throughout the Mediterranean in an effort to secure their trade routes and solidify their influence. Sardinia, a land rich with resources, was one of the first places that Carthage set its eyes on. Carthage successfully placed the city under its control by the late 6th century BCE. Spain also felt the influence of Carthage, as Carthaginian settlers established new trade centers along the Iberian coast.

Sicily witnessed the emergence of Phoenician trading posts and colonies along the western coast of the island beginning in the 8th century BCE. However, these early settlements were built primarily as commercial hubs to facilitate trade between the Phoenician cities and the western Mediterranean. It was only when Phoenicia's power declined in the 6th century BCE that Carthage began to inherit control over the settlements in Sicily. Sicily was a key strategic location (it was close to both Italy and North Africa), so Carthaginians planned to expand their wings on the island even more.

This brought the Carthaginians into conflicts with the Greek colonies stationed on the eastern and southern parts of the island. The Sicilian Wars were fought between Carthage and Greek city-states (particularly Syracuse) over the control of Sicily. The result of this war was mixed for Carthage. While Carthage managed to secure and expand its influence over western Sicily, it failed to fully realize its goal of controlling the entire island. The Greeks managed to hold onto the eastern part of the island. Later on, during the Punic Wars, Sicily was yet again made the trophy for the victor of the war. After losing the war in 241 BCE, Carthage was forced to retreat and relinquish its holdings in Sicily to Rome.

Despite their eventual defeat at the hands of the Romans, Carthage's military was a force to be reckoned with. Unlike the Romans, whose legionnaires consisted of their own citizens, the Carthaginian military was primarily a mercenary force. The city enlisted soldiers from across the Mediterranean and beyond. Carthage was even able to hire troops from Iberia and Greece. The Carthaginians also had powerful alliances with the Numidian tribes of North Africa, particularly the Masaesyli and the Massylii. These Berber tribes were best known for their impressive cavalry and eventually became the most important part of the Carthaginian military force. The Carthaginian generals were skilled in commanding this mix of mercenary forces. In wars, they often engaged their enemies using a combination of cavalry, light infantry, and, later on, war elephants.

However, the navy was considered the true backbone of Carthaginian power. Since the Mediterranean was Carthage's primary region for both trade and war, naval supremacy was essential. The Carthaginians' naval legacy stemmed from the Phoenicians, who were exceptional shipbuilders. The Carthaginians built some of the finest ships of their era. They were often modeled after Phoenician designs, with their speed and maneuverability greatly improved for battle.

The Carthaginian quinqueremes were Carthage's most powerful warships. The name quinquereme came from its best feature: these warships had three rows of oars with five rowers. Because of this, the quinquereme was able to sail at a greater speed than other ships. The warship's rams, typically made of bronze, were used to smash or even cleave enemy ships. Given its size, the quinquereme could carry a large number of soldiers and catapults.

However, one of the most intriguing voyages that the Carthaginians ever took was in 520 BCE. Led by Hanno the Navigator under the order of the Carthaginian government, his task was to explore and colonize parts of West Africa. The scale of this particular expedition was immense. Hanno was given sixty vessels to command, carrying a total of thirty thousand men and women.

With all the preparations ready, Hanno and his fleet left Carthage and sailed westward. He passed through the Pillars of Hercules and into the Atlantic Ocean. Along the way, the Carthaginians successfully founded several settlements, leaving behind groups of colonists to establish new cities. Unfortunately for us, the exact location of these colonies remains debated. Some claim that Cerne and Thymiaterium (located in present-day Morocco) were among the colonies established by Hanno and the Carthaginians. Nevertheless, it is safe to assume that this expedition opened the door to greater exploration of the African coast.

Hanno pushed farther south from Carthage, which took the Carthaginians along the West African coast. Possibly in modern-day Mauritania (not to be confused with the ancient Kingdom of Mauretania) or Senegal, they encountered a range of wildlife. Crocodiles and hippopotamuses were known to some extent by those in North Africa. However, these animals were far more common in the southern regions of sub-Saharan Africa compared to North Africa. Encountering these creatures in larger numbers along the rivers of West Africa would have been a thrilling experience for the Carthaginians. Hippopotamuses, in particular, were known for their size and aggression. So, their voyage in this region was far from a walk in the park.

The most dramatic encounter came when Hanno and the Carthaginians reached what he referred to as the "Horn of the South." Scholars believe this could have been the region around Sierra Leone or perhaps farther down the coast toward Gabon. According to Hanno's account, it was here that the Carthaginians encountered a group of large and aggressive creatures. Hanno had never seen these creatures before in his life, and he described them as wild and rather hairy human-like beasts. While Hanno called them *gorillae,* we know the creature today as gorillas.

It is also widely believed that the Carthaginians managed to capture three female gorillas. However, the great apes quickly turned aggressive, causing havoc. The crew had no choice but to kill the gorillas. The Carthaginians then skinned them and brought the pelts back to Carthage.

Of course, Hanno and the Carthaginians encountered various African people along the way. While some extended their welcome, offering supplies and sharing their knowledge with the Carthaginians, there were those who were hostile.

Although the Carthaginians met dozens of challenges, Hanno continued to push southward. Historians and scholars are still unsure of the exact length of Hanno's voyage, but many believe that he reached at least as far as present-day Sierra Leone. Others suggest that he might have gone farther into Gabon. Experts estimate that he covered 2,600 miles of coastline; to put this into perspective, it would be like sailing from the western coast of Portugal all the way to the southern tip of Norway. This was very impressive for the time since ancient sailors had to rely on sailing by the stars, the coastline, and nature, like wind patterns.

Although Carthage was said to have been founded by Queen Dido, historical accounts suggest that the city was never a monarchy. Instead, Carthage operated under a republican government—a system that was somewhat similar to the one used in Rome, except for a few unique features. At the top were two officials known as suffetes. Similar to Roman consuls, these two officials were elected annually. They held both executive and judicial authority. Their primary duty was, of course, to oversee the city's entire administration. The suffetes could also propose decisions to the Senate.

Like the Roman Republic, the Senate was considered the true powerhouse of Carthaginian politics. Composed of the city's elites, the Senate functioned as the primary legislative body. Decisions and policies related to war, diplomacy, and financial matters were debated among the senators. Unsurprisingly, the senior officials—typically rich aristocrats or highly influenced military leaders—were the ones who held significant influence within the Senate.

Complementing the Senate was a popular assembly known as the 'm (possibly pronounced as "ham"). Meaning "the people," this body would meet in the city's market square, where they would vote on issues presented by the suffetes and the Senate. The popular assembly was responsible for electing officials, including the suffetes themselves, priests, treasurers, and even military commanders. How their voting system worked, however, remains a mystery to us.

Citizenship was reserved for free Carthaginian men, though those from elite families held the most influence. They had the right to vote, participate in the assembly, and hold public office. Women, foreigners, and, of course, slaves generally could not enjoy these privileges.

Although some scholars suggest there was a second tier of citizens, no one has been able to fully confirm this.

Similar to many other empires, kingdoms, and nations, the problem of corruption was difficult to overcome. Bribery was common in Carthage. Money would be used to secure votes, get favorable decisions, or access high-ranking positions. When the famous Hannibal Barca was first elected suffete, one of his main focuses was to cut down the corruption that was crippling the city's finances. He introduced several reforms aimed at reducing the power of the corrupt elites. While ensuring public revenue was collected more efficiently, Hannibal also imposed anti-corruption measures, putting a halt to state officials from illegally drawing money from state funds. Through these efforts and reforms, Carthage was able to pay off its war indemnity to Rome faster.

Religion was also deeply embedded in Carthaginian life. Since the founders of Carthage were from Tyre, it is not surprising that the city's religious scene bore great similarities with Tyre. The Carthaginians were polytheists, meaning they believed in a pantheon of gods. However, the city's most important deity was known as Baal Hammon (interpreted by scholars as the Lord of the Brazier). As both the king of the gods and the mighty god of fertility, Baal Hammon was worshiped so that the Carthaginians could enjoy the fertility of their land. The Carthaginians also held the goddess known as Tanit in high regard. Representing love, fertility, and motherhood, Tanit was believed to be the consort of Baal Hammon. However, Tanit eventually superseded Baal Hammon in importance in later years to the point where her name was typically placed before Baal Hammon in monuments built in the city.

Like the Greeks and the Romans, the Carthaginians performed rituals and sacrifices to appease their gods. Perhaps one of the most controversial rituals of the Carthaginian religion was the child sacrifice performed in the city's sacred precinct, the Tophet. The Greek historian Diodorus pictured a vivid scene of this horrifying practice. More commonly done during a time of crisis, it was said that these children were offered to the gods in exchange for a certain favor or protection from harm. It is said that the child was publicly presented or sometimes paraded before they were sacrificed. The child was then placed into the arms of a heated bronze statue before being buried in a small urn.

What remains of the Carthaginian Tophet.[29]

However, whether or not this ritual was ever performed remains a mystery, as the claim has been increasingly challenged by modern scholars. The Tophet did contain urns filled with cremated remains of infants and young children, but scholars argued that the Tophet might have been a necropolis for the young who died from natural causes rather than a place for ritualistic sacrifice.

Chapter 6 – The Lost Tribes of the Sahara Desert

The Sahara is the world's largest hot desert. Spread across North Africa, the region consists of endless dunes, rocky plateaus, and salt pans (the remnants of the ancient seabed). However, the Sahara has not always been a land of merciless heat and sand. It was a much greener place thousands of years ago, with a landscape full of rivers, lakes, and lush grasslands. From fossil evidence and rock art preserved by the passage of time, it has been revealed that the Sahara once teemed with life. Giraffes, elephants, and hippos roamed the region freely, and the humans were blessed with abundant resources, enough for both settlement and growth.

Regardless of this greener climate, settling in the Sahara was not without its challenges, even back then. Its rugged terrain and intense seasonal variations could only be endured by those who were resilient enough. When the desert began to face climate change, its rivers began to dry up, and its once-fertile plains eventually turned to sand. These environmental changes shaped the stories of the ancient tribes that inhabited the Sahara. Many thrived, bringing their name onto the world stage. Others, however, only had their luck last for a few centuries before their decline and eventual disappearance. These lost tribes left only traces of their existence in the sands for us to uncover.

The Aterians and the Capsians

Two of the earliest inhabitants of the Sahara were the Aterians and the Capsians. These two ancient cultures flourished long before the desert's transformation. The Aterians emerged as early as 145,000 years ago. Named after the Bir el Ater site in Algeria, the Aterians primarily lived off the land. With their stone tools, these people hunted big game and gathered edible plants. They also fished in the rivers and lakes that once dotted North Africa, using nothing more than early bone hooks and simple traps. Their surroundings were greener than they are today, but they still needed a deep knowledge of nature's rhythms in order to make the most of the region's resources.

As time went on, the Aterians became a thing of the past and were succeeded by the Capsians. Arriving around 10,000 BCE, the Capsians brought new advancements to the Sahara. Early signs of agriculture and animal domestication could be seen with their arrival. In contrast to the Aterians, who focused on hunting and foraging, the Capsians cultivated wild grains and managed herds. They also lived in semi-permanent settlements, although their dwellings were rather simple. The Capsians' stone tools and other decorative objects also appeared more advanced than the Aterians. Capsian art, typically painted on rocks, still remains today; they depict different scenes, from daily life to spiritual beliefs.

However, the mentions of the Aterians would disappear when the Sahara's climate shifted. The Capsians also eventually vanished, though much later. With the rivers drying and the vegetation gradually disappearing, the people found it hard to sustain themselves. While some scholars suggest they might have migrated to more hospitable areas to survive, others believe they disappeared entirely, becoming a part of the chapter called the lost tribes of the Sahara.

The Garamantes

The Garamantes inhabited the Fezzan region in modern-day southwestern Libya. Emerging sometime around 500 BCE, the Garamantes are credited as one of the Sahara's most remarkable ancient cultures by archaeologists. They transformed their arid homeland into a flourishing civilization, and this civilization was said to have developed agricultural techniques that were ahead of their time. Known as oasis agriculture, this technique involved harnessing underground water reservoirs to support their extensive farming.

To make this innovation work, the Garamantes used the foggara, a series of underground tunnels that channeled water from deep aquifers to the surface. Through these sets of tunnels, the people were able to provide their crops with a steady supply of water. Wheat, barley, dates, and grapes were successfully cultivated despite the almost inhospitable landscape of the Sahara Desert.

With this agricultural success, the Garamantes managed to expand their influence across the continent, especially in trade. They eventually established themselves as key intermediaries in trans-Saharan trade, connecting the Mediterranean world with Saharan and sub-Saharan Africa. Day and night, the Garamantes welcomed caravans loaded with gold, other exotic goods, and slaves. They traded with various ancient powers, from Carthage to Egypt and even Rome. In return for their prized desert goods, the Garamantes got their hands on metals, various luxury items, and knowledge from distant cultures. Over time, the Garamantes managed to position themselves as a powerful and influential society in the heart of the Sahara.

The ruins of Garama (Germa), a major city built by the Garamantes.[80]

Research claims the Garamantes established eight major cities. However, it was their capital city, Garama (known today as Germa, located 150 kilometers west of modern-day Sabha), that became a melting pot of commerce and cultural exchange. The city was home to many grand buildings and structures, from nearly impenetrable fortifications to dozens of workshops, residential homes, granaries, bustling marketplaces, and temples. With evidence suggesting that Garama was once an impressive urban city, it is not surprising to learn that the Garamantes had a well-organized social structure, with ruling elites and noble families at the top of the hierarchy.

Despite the limited information and evidence available about their religious beliefs, many scholars agree that the Garamantes worshiped a variety of gods. North African gods might have been included in their pantheon of gods, and they likely worshiped foreign deities introduced to them through trade and cultural exchange. The ancient Greek historian Herodotus mentioned in his *Histories* of a certain god crucial to the Garamantes' beliefs, said to be known as Ammon—possibly the same god as the Egyptians' Amun. Herodotus claimed the deity was associated with the ram and the sun and was considered a benevolent god who looked after those who worshiped him.

The Garamantes worshiped other local gods and goddesses whose names are forever lost to history. We can be sure that these deities were associated with natural phenomena, such as water and fertility. It is believed the Garamantes eventually adopted the worship of the Greek god Demeter at some point.

The Garamantes continued to rise, with their power reaching its peak during the 2nd and 3rd centuries CE. By this time, Garama alone had a population of four thousand, while another six thousand lived in villages scattered within a five-kilometer radius. This was also the period when they were almost continuously in conflict with the Roman Empire to the north. The Garamantes were very bold; they often conducted raids across Rome's African frontier. They would launch surprise attacks and retreat to the safety of the desert, knowing the Romans were still unfamiliar with the harsh environment.

In 203 CE, when Rome was ruled by Emperor Septimius Severus, Garama fell; it was captured by the Romans. However, this was not the end of the Garamantes, as the emperor soon abandoned the city.

The Sahara was already a desert by the time of the Garamantes. Yet, long-term environmental changes, including the drying of oases and declining groundwater, made sustaining life increasingly difficult. Other factors, including the fall of the Roman Empire, the rise of Christianity, and the rise of Islam, led to the Garamantes eventually disappearing from historical records.

The Gaetulians

The Gaetulians inhabited the rough regions of the central Sahara, primarily in modern-day Algeria and certain parts of Morocco. Considered to be an ancient Berber-speaking people, the Gaetulians lived a nomadic lifestyle. The classical historian Strabo wrote about the Gaetulians. He described them as living independently. These people were often divided into small and highly mobile groups. They moved from one location to another in search of resources and water. Once they had found the perfect location, these people would build fortified encampments and other defensive structures, perhaps to protect themselves from rival tribes and secure a safe outpost for trade. Remnants of such structures, including stone enclosures, have been found by archaeologists.

Despite the challenges of the inhospitable landscape, these people thrived. The Roman writer Pliny the Elder once described the Gaetulians as one of the most resilient people he had ever seen. The Roman also claimed they were exceptional horsemen and warriors who were undoubtedly well adapted to the rugged terrain of the region. This mastery over horses eventually became a central part of the Gaetulians' identity and influence later on.

Pliny the Elder, in his writings from *Natural History*, provides us with an insight into the Gaetulians' fierce identity; he even noted they were "wild and warlike." The Gaetulian warriors were experts in fighting; they were often recruited to fight under different banners. The Carthaginians highly valued the Gaetulians' renowned mastery over horses and weapons and recruited these warriors during the Punic Wars. Their agility and precious knowledge of the desert benefited the Carthaginians greatly during the conflict.

However, spotting these warriors among the Carthaginians was simple. The Gaetulian warriors were known for their distinctive attire. While Carthaginian infantry marched wearing heavy armor, the Gaetulians preferred to charge into battle wearing leather hides.

According to Pliny, they were known for their leatherworking. Their leather goods were not only crucial in wars but also highly valued in trade.

Since the Gaetulians, like a few other tribes of the Sahara, acted as intermediaries between sub-Saharan Africa and the Mediterranean world, it is not surprising that they had frequent contact with various powerful kingdoms and empires of the time. Trade enriched the Gaetulians, and their contact with the Carthaginians and Romans allowed for a degree of cultural exchange that eventually influenced their economy and lifestyle. The Gaetulians somewhat integrated into Carthaginian and Roman societies as time passed by, but when Rome launched their mighty expansion into North Africa, the Gaetulians' influence gradually waned.

As Rome began to establish its own routes and fortify its many provinces North Africa, the Gaetulians' position as trade intermediaries declined. By 17 CE, the Musulamii tribe (a Gaetulian sub-tribe) retaliated against the Romans. This led to one of the largest wars in the region of modern-day Algeria (the area was known as Roman Africa at the time). The Gaetulians and the neighboring Garamantes joined forces with the Musulamii to fight against the Romans. However, the Romans proved to be too powerful. With the defeat of the Musulamii, mentions of the Gaetulians disappeared from Roman military records.

The Nasamones

Meanwhile, in the eastern part of the Sahara, specifically parts of present-day Libya along the edges of the Cyrenaica region, the world saw the emergence of another ancient nomadic Berber tribe: the Nasamones. These people lived near the oasis and relied on date palm cultivation. Dates, small-scale herding, and gathering supported their way of life.

Pliny the Elder also mentioned the Nasamones. The Roman portrayed them as people who were well adapted to the desert's demands. Pliny also talked about their interactions with nearby Greek and Roman settlements, proving that the Nasamones were not entirely isolated. They engaged in trade, exchanging goods like dates and hides. By doing this, the Nasamones were able to be introduced to elements of Mediterranean culture, although they preferred to retain their own customs and beliefs.

Herodotus, on the other hand, claimed the Nasamones were skilled diviners. According to the ancient historian, the Nasamones had a unique ability to locate water. They used this gift to guide traders and caravans through the merciless desert. Because of this divination practice, which was likely due to their exceptional understanding of the land and weather patterns rather than being some psychic gift, the Nasamones were considered valuable allies, especially to those passing along the trans-Saharan trade routes.

Of course, the Nasamones were not only skilled in desert survival. They were also formidable fighters. They used war chariots drawn by four horses, which allowed them to traverse and fight across the challenging terrain with speed and agility. The Nasamones had a history of raiding neighboring territories, especially the Greek colonies in Cyrenaica. They rarely saw eye to eye with the Greeks, and the Nasamones never refrained from launching bold attacks against them. However, the Greeks were not known to back down; the Nasamones were eventually defeated in battles, suffering heavy losses.

When Rome's influence began to spread through North Africa, the Nasamones were among those brought under their rule. This, unsurprisingly, led to tensions. Things went south when Roman officials began extorting money from them. The Nasamones revolted, but luck was not on their side, as they faced suppression from the Romans. They later became vassals of the Eastern Roman Empire and maintained a level of autonomy under the Romans' careful gaze. However, for unknown reasons, the Nasamones faded from historical records after the 6th century CE, leaving their fate for us to wonder.

The Libu

According to ancient Egyptian records, the Libu inhabited areas west of the Nile Delta. Referred to as "Libyans" by the Egyptians, they were a powerful force in North African history, with their presence dating back as early as the 13th century BCE. Despite being almost constantly mentioned by the ancient Egyptians, their interactions were not always peaceful. The Libu were seen as a source of influence and a threat, especially during the era of the New Kingdom. Pharaohs from that period, particularly Merneptah and Ramesses III, often clashed with the Libu. Descriptions from stelae detail full-scale wars against the Libu, who attempted to push into Egyptian territories in the Nile Delta. The Egyptians also depicted the Libu as fierce warriors and skilled herdsmen.

They wore leather garments and feathered headdresses.

Apart from being exceptional warriors and soldiers, the Libu was thought to have a highly organized semi-nomadic lifestyle. Their society was organized around a tribal structure, with chieftains placed at the top. The Libu were predominantly pastoral, often focusing on cattle and goat herding. As desert-dwellers, the Libu possessed extensive knowledge of the desert. They had the ability to traverse across the Sahara's demanding landscape with little difficulty. Their expertise in managing the desert's scarce resources also gave them an advantage in maintaining control over their territories and played a crucial role in their conflicts and trade interactions with other civilizations, such as Carthage, Egypt, and Rome.

It is safe to say the Libu people's influence could be felt across North Africa; they are considered to have been one of the foundational groups that contributed to the Berber identity that still exists today. Archaeological findings suggest a linguistic and cultural continuity between the Libu and later Berber communities; there are similarities in their languages, social structures, and customs. Evidence from pottery styles, traditional attire, and burial practices also linked the Libu to later Berber tribes. Even today, certain aspects of Berber dress, such as leather garments and specific patterns, bear a resemblance to ancient Libyan attire depicted in Egyptian reliefs.

However, as centuries passed, the Libu faced the same fate as the other tribes included in this chapter. Their prominence eventually faded when the world saw the rise of more powerful empires, such as Carthage and, later, Rome, which successfully dominated the North African coast.

Chapter 7 – Ancient Berber Kingdoms: Numidia and Mauretania

It was 203 BCE, and the Second Punic War had escalated to new heights. The conflict had brought a particular figure named Masinissa to the plains of Cirta. The Numidian king sat atop his steed, his eyes focused on the campfires flickering in the distance. Masinissa was not in the mood to sleep that night. His mind was fixed on the battle that would take place tomorrow, as it would determine the fate of the Numidians. Masinissa and his Roman allies were to meet the army of Syphax, another king of Numidia, who, like himself, saw a vision to unite the kingdom under one banner.

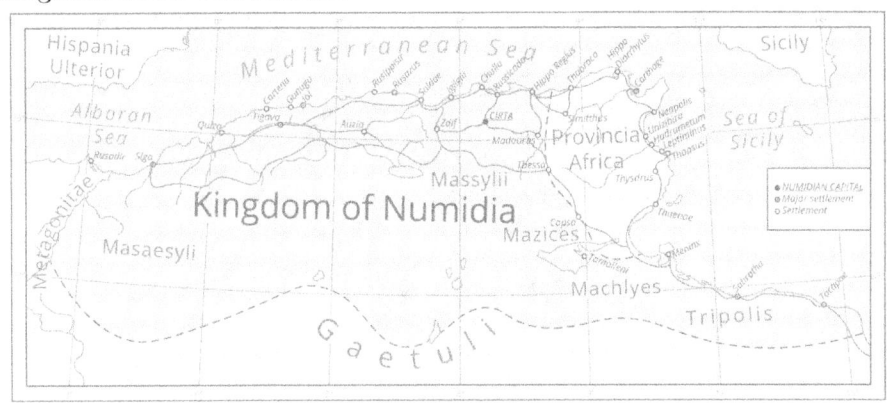

Map of Numidia after the Punic Wars.[81]

However, the war was not the only thing that occupied Masinissa's mind. He also had the face of a certain woman lingering in his mind. Named Sophonisba, she was supposed to be united with Masinissa under the bond of matrimony. Unfortunately, war, alliances, and fate had intervened in their lives. In the end, Sophonisba's hand in marriage went to Syphax.

Masinissa planned to rely on his cavalry. The might of the Numidian cavalry was known across the Mediterranean; in fact, this was Masinissa's greatest asset. Each Numidian rider possessed skills on their mount that no one else could compete with. They rode light. Instead of donning shining heavy armor, their protection was a leopard skin slung across their shoulders. They also carried a small, often round shield made of leather. Perhaps the most distinguishable feature of the Numidian cavalry was how they rode their horses. They used neither reins nor saddles. Instead of using bridles, they guided their horses by using ropes looped around their necks. Since their horses were typically smaller in size compared to other horses of that time (their horses were the ancestors of the species known as the Berber horse), the Numidian cavalry was able to move faster over longer distances. As for their weapons, they used javelins and a short sword.

The cavalry's reputation grew even bigger in 201 BCE since they turned the tide in the Battle of Zama. With the cavalry by their side, the Romans had succeeded in defeating Hannibal, the Carthaginian general who had long been a dangerous thorn in the Roman Republic's military efforts.

A drawing of a Numidian cavalry member. [89]

The Early Days of Numidia

Everything has a beginning. Long before the rise of kings and warriors like Masinissa and Syphax, Numidia (present-day Algeria) was a land of nomads. For centuries, the deserts and the wild hills of North Africa became home to the Berber tribes (also known as the Imazighen). They lived off the land, hunting and herding animals to sustain their lifestyle. They had no central authority. Each tribe was independent. They were ruled by their own chieftain, and loyalties were often rooted in bloodlines and ancestral traditions. Because of this, they had no unifying force to bind them together.

One of the first external powers to have engaged with these Berber tribes was the Phoenicians, who established the city of Carthage along the North African coast. When the great city grew, turning itself into a powerful maritime empire, the Carthaginians thought it was best to form alliances with the Berber tribes. Through the support of these tribes, Carthage was able to enlist the Berber warriors into their ranks and traded various goods with them, such as grains, livestock, and metals. Of course, this benefitted the Carthaginians, but this relationship also planted the seeds of change among the Berbers. Perhaps witnessing Carthage's wealth and growing power, the Berber leaders finally realized the importance of unity—especially when they found themselves increasingly involved in the Punic Wars.

When the Second Punic War broke out in 218 BCE, two of the most powerful Berber tribes—Maesulii in the east and the Masaesyli in the west—eventually rose as regional powers. While the Maesulii were under the leadership of Masinissa, the Masaesyli were led by Syphax. Both leaders envisioned a united Numidia, but their paths diverged dramatically as they became deeply embroiled in the war between Carthage and Rome. Syphax chose to ally with Carthage. He saw this alliance as a golden opportunity for him to expand his influence across North Africa.

Masinissa, on the other hand, chose another path, as he had already seen the flaws of Carthaginian power firsthand. As the son of a Numidian chieftain who had allied with Carthage, Masinissa had experience fighting alongside the empire in the early years of the Second Punic War. However, Masinissa viewed Carthage's heavy reliance on mercenaries as a flaw. Combined with the empire's internal political strife, Masinissa saw the possibility of Rome defeating Carthage and becoming the most powerful force in the ancient world. The Numidian king decided to switch sides. He believed his allegiance to the Roman Republic could lead to a united Numidia that could stand independently.

Coin with an image of King Masinissa. [88]

His defection set in motion a conflict between himself and the other Numidian leader, Syphax. In the early stages of their rivalry, Syphax succeeded in gaining the upper hand. He overran Masinissa's lands and managed to force the Maesulii king into exile. It was only when the Romans, led by General Publius Cornelius Scipio, invaded North Africa that Masinissa was given another chance to restore his reputation. Together with the Roman forces under Scipio, Masinissa and his Numidian warriors fought against Syphax and his Carthaginian allies at the Battle of Utica in 203 BCE. Although Syphax was defeated, he managed to flee back to his capital, Cirta. The two Numidian kings would clash swords once more at the Battle of Cirta.

The Battle of Cirta

Dawn finally came, and the vast plains to the east of Cirta were immediately brought to life with the sounds of preparations. When the battle commenced, Masinissa's cavalry rode their unsaddled horses at great speed. They had been training hard for this very moment, sharpening their skills through countless skirmishes and battles. In contrast to Syphax's heavily armored forces, which had to charge in their bulky gear, the Numidians wanted to leverage their swift movements to incapacitate their enemies. They darted in and out of combat as if they were fleeting shadows.

Syphax's army, which was supported by Carthaginian infantry, outnumbered Masinissa's forces. However, in Masinissa's eyes, these numbers meant nothing; he knew that his troops' superior tactics could turn the tide. With their expertise in the art of hit-and-run attacks, Masinissa's cavalry hurled their javelins with extreme accuracy before retreating beyond the reach of their enemies. The Numidian cavalry also used the terrain to their advantage. It was clear that Syphax's troops were struggling to keep up.

The bloodshed continued until midday. Masinissa's horsemen continued to dart across the battlefield and drive deep into Syphax's lines. Once they spread terror among their enemies, they retreated into the hills, forcing Syphax's forces to stretch thin. The Numidians under Masinissa seemed untouchable, and no matter how hard Syphax's cavalry pressed on, they failed to catch up to them. Their heavy armor protected them from instant death by blades and arrows, but they were also weighed down by their equipment to the point where they constantly found themselves outmaneuvered by their enemy at every turn. The morale of Syphax's men continued to plummet, especially when the Roman legionnaires made their advance.

Syphax attempted to rally his men, but destiny had another idea. His horse was shot, and the Numidian king fell to the ground, only to be captured by his enemy. There was no escape for Syphax. He was brought to Rome and paraded through the streets as part of the Romans' victory procession. The Numidian king was placed under house arrest in the town of Tibur (modern-day Tivoli), where he was reduced to a prisoner of war. He died shortly after the end of the Second Punic War, possibly sometime around 202 BCE.

As for Masinissa, he was hailed as the undisputed ruler of Numidia. Even though victory was his, Masinissa entered the city of Cirta with a heavy heart. Inside the capital city, he laid eyes on Sophonisba, who stood tall despite her circumstances. Rome demanded her as a war prize, given her direct ties with Syphax. However, Masinissa did not have the heart to hand her over. He knew what awaited his lover should he hand her to the Romans; Sophonisba would be paraded through the streets of Rome, reduced to only a symbol of conquest. Torn between his duty to his ally and his lingering love for Sophonisba, Masinissa knew he had to make a decision. The Numidian king granted her a way out. He gave her a cup of poison, allowing Sophonisba to take her own life with dignity. His lover eventually breathed her last breath in his arms, a scene that would haunt him forever.

The death of Sophonisba.⁵⁴

Despite being filled with sorrow, Masinissa turned his focus to Numidia. No longer a land of nomadic tribes with its people divided and vulnerable, Masinissa worked to secure his kingdom's future. Given Numidia's strategic location—it was situated between the Mediterranean coast and sub-Saharan Africa—one of his highest priority tasks was to strengthen the kingdom's trade network.

Under his leadership, Numidia transformed into a thriving center of agriculture. Since Numidia's lands were fertile, Masinissa took steps to modernize agricultural practices. Various irrigation techniques were introduced to further improve the productivity of the land. This ensured that the kingdom could not only feed its own people but also the armies of its Roman allies. Soon, dozens of estates emerged where wheat and olive were produced in abundance. Olives were pressed and turned into one of the kingdom's most valuable exports: olive oil. These were just some of the goods that became the backbone of the kingdom's economy. They were typically exported to Rome and Carthage. Gold, other precious metals, and various luxury goods from sub-Saharan Africa were also commonly traded along Numidia's trade routes. Numidia gained immense wealth as a result, allowing Masinissa to build more fortified cities, roads, and other infrastructure needed to make the kingdom one of the important players in the ancient world.

Despite experiencing modernization and external influences, Numidia never strayed too far from the Berber culture. For centuries, they lived off the land, so it was not surprising that the daily lives of the Numidians after the war still revolved around the land. The people often became farmers, often cultivating wheat and olives, or herders who tended to flocks of goats and cattle. The Numidian language, written in the Tifinagh script, was also retained to display their identity. Although Punic and Latin were typically used in official matters, the Numidians continued to speak and write in their own language. Art in the kingdom blended Berber traditions with external influences, such as those from Carthage, Rome, and Egypt. The Numidians were also skilled in craftsmanship. They were experts in pottery, metalwork, and other intricate leather goods, which were often used in their daily lives and religious ceremonies.

Of course, like many other ancient civilizations, religion was a central part of Numidian life. In fact, this was where the blending of cultures was most evident. Ever since the earliest of times, the Berbers worshiped gods related to the sun, the moon, the earth, and the mountains. Usually, their religious rituals were held in sacred groves or at the bases of mountains. Here, offerings were made to please the gods. A certain ritual involving libations (the pouring of liquids, such as wine or oil) as offerings to the spirits of the land was especially common among the Numidians. Often performed in sacred groves or at springs, this ceremony was done to appease the earth and the spirits believed to inhabit it. Masinissa himself might have partaken in such rituals, especially when he was in need of divine support for his political moves or military campaigns.

However, due to the long-standing Carthaginian influence and Numidia's geographic and cultural proximity to Carthage, the people began to adopt the practices of the Phoenician gods, including Baal and Tanit. Of course, this did not entirely erase their centuries-old religious beliefs. The statues of these foreign deities could often be seen standing alongside the old Berber gods.

The tomb of Masinissa.[85]

It is safe to conclude that Numidia flourished under Masinissa. It turned into one of the most powerful kingdoms in North Africa. His vision for independence and unity had become a reality. Unfortunately, this would not last for too long. Despite having forged strong ties with the Roman Republic, Numidia would soon meet the same fate as many other smaller states that happened to be in the way of Rome's path to glory.

Numidia and Rome would eventually be at each other's throats beginning in 112 BCE. This was when Masinissa's grandson, Jugurtha, began to challenge Rome's authority. He waged a long and stubborn resistance against the Romans in what is known to us today as the Jugurthine War (112-105 BCE). Numidia's independence became a thing of the past when Jugurtha was finally captured by the Romans and executed. Numidia was turned into a client kingdom under Roman influence. Since a client kingdom was semi-autonomous, Numidia retained its local rulers but lost much of its sovereignty.

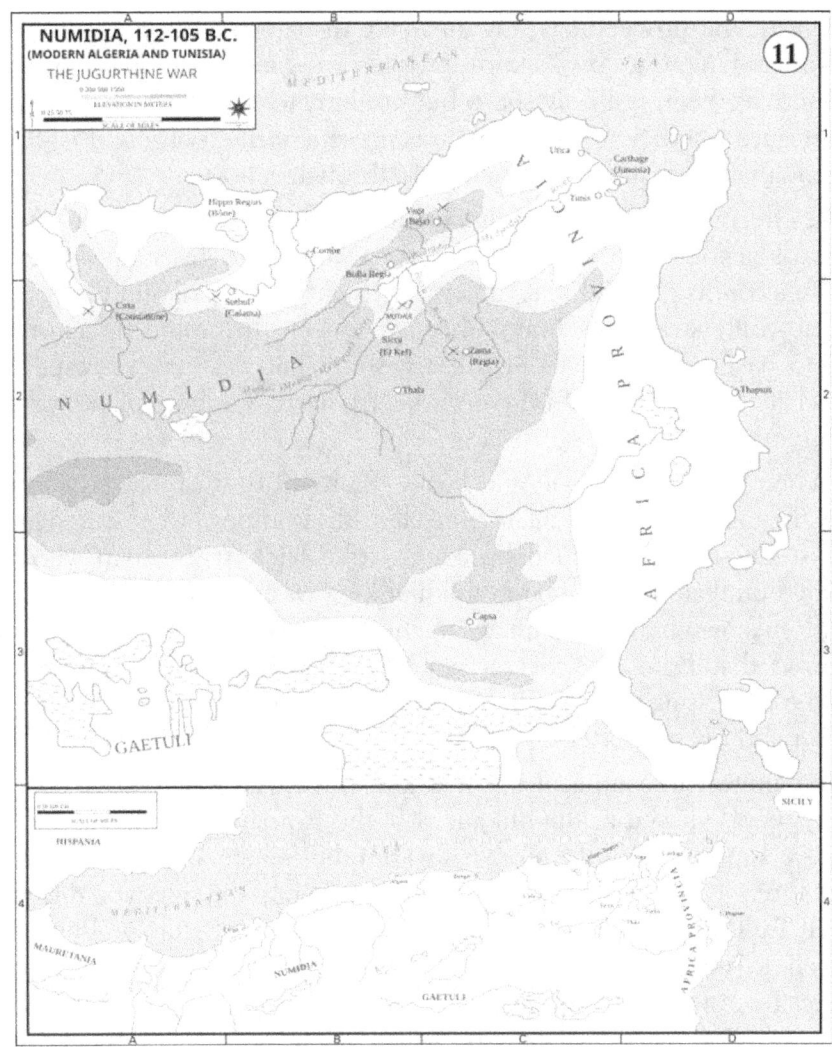

Numidia between 112 and 105 BCE.[36]

Juba I and Numidia's Annexation into the Roman Empire

In 60 BCE, the Numidian crown passed to Juba I. Juba I held deep resentment toward a certain famous Roman general: Julius Caesar.

It all began before Juba rose to the throne when Caesar served as an advocate in Rome. A few businessmen had reported their dissatisfaction against the reigning king of Numidia at the time, Hiempsal II (Juba's father). They accused him of reneging on debts or agreements. The case was brought before the Roman court, and Julius Caesar represented the businessmen.

During the proceedings, Caesar made disparaging remarks about the Numidian king. Caesar was known for his arrogance, but his rhetoric was said to have been not only sharp but insulting to the Numidian royals. It was unsure whether or not Juba I was present at the trial, but it is safe to assume that he was aware of the insults through reports.

As the prince of the Numidian throne, Juba I would have viewed Caesar's actions as a direct and personal affront to his family's honor. Some accounts claimed that Juba was present at the trial and that Caesar did not only smear his honor through speech; the future dictator was said to have pulled Juba's beard, a gesture that was very disrespectful, especially in Berber culture where beards were symbols of honor and manhood.

When the Roman Civil War broke out in 49 BCE, Juba was eager to take the opportunity to align himself with Pompey, who was fighting against Caesar. Juba hoped he could strike back at the man who had greatly humiliated him. The Numidian king wasted no time in using his kingdom's resources and military might to support Pompey's cause. Juba believed that Pompey's victory would avenge his personal grievances, and he also sought to shield Numidia from the growing influence of Caesar and his supporters.

For quite some time, it seemed as if Juba's gamble would pay off. Pompey was viewed as the old guard of the Roman Republic, so he had massive support from the Romans within the Senate and commanded a large force. Unfortunately for the Numidian king, the tide would turn in 48 BCE. Pompey was defeated by Caesar at the Battle of Pharsalus. Forced to flee, Pompey arrived on the shores of Alexandria, Egypt, where he met his demise under the order of the young pharaoh, Ptolemy XIII. Juba's nightmare began to turn into reality; Caesar's uncontested rise to power had just begun.

The Battle of Thapsus and Juba's Downfall

With Pompey's defeat, Juba found himself in a precarious position. Having openly supported Caesar's greatest enemy, he knew it was only a matter of time before Numidia would face the full force of the Roman legions.

In 46 BCE, Caesar took his forces to North Africa, where he fought the remnants of Pompey's supporters. Juba, alongside the Roman senator and military commander Metellus Scipio, gathered what remained of the anti-Caesarian forces to meet Julius Caesar at the Battle of Thapsus. Juba's forces were well trained and highly experienced from decades of skirmishes. However, they were clearly unmatched by the sheer size and discipline of Caesar's legions.

Caesar and his experienced veterans easily overwhelmed the combined forces of Juba and Scipio. Despite their efforts to repel Caesar's attack, the Numidians were quickly routed and forced into a chaotic retreat. Well aware that the battle was lost, Juba fled the battlefield. He was unwilling to face the humiliation of capture; the king could not imagine himself in shackles and being paraded along the streets of Rome. He and another one of his Roman allies, Marcus Petreius, sought refuge on an estate near Zama. However, knowing that there was no way out, the two resorted to ending their lives. Instead of poisoning each other, the two engaged in a duel. Petreius ended up killing Juba. Petrius, with the help of a slave, then proceeded to kill himself afterward.

With the death of Juba I, Numidia lost all hope of independence. Numidia was turned into a Roman province.

Juba II and Mauretania

Juba I had a son, the only heir to the Numidian throne. Known simply as Juba II, Julius Caesar took the young Numidian prince to Rome (he was probably between four and six years old at this time). In the Eternal City, he was raised under Roman care. He received a Roman education, learning about Roman customs and Greek and Latin literature. Juba II was extremely dedicated to his studies and rose to become one of Rome's most educated citizens; he even wrote his first work by the time he turned twenty.

When Caesar died, Juba II was raised by Octavian (later known as Emperor Augustus). Juba II was said to have been loyal to Octavian. He accompanied the future emperor on various military missions. The Numidian prince even fought alongside Octavian in the Battle of Actium against Mark Antony. Octavian rewarded Juba II greatly. He was restored as the king of Numidia and appointed as the client king of Mauritania, a neighboring kingdom on the western coast of North Africa.

Mauretania, located along the Atlantic coast of North Africa (covering present-day northern Morocco and southward to the Atlas Mountains), was known as a kingdom of immense wealth and strategic importance. Much like its neighbor Numidia, Mauretania was a vital hub for trade between sub-Saharan Africa and the Mediterranean. Gold, ivory, and spices from various African regions passed through Mauretania's trade networks and were brought into the markets of Carthage, Rome, and even Greece. Mauretania imported all kinds of luxury goods from these regions, including fine pottery and wine, which were common staples in the palaces of the kingdom's elite.

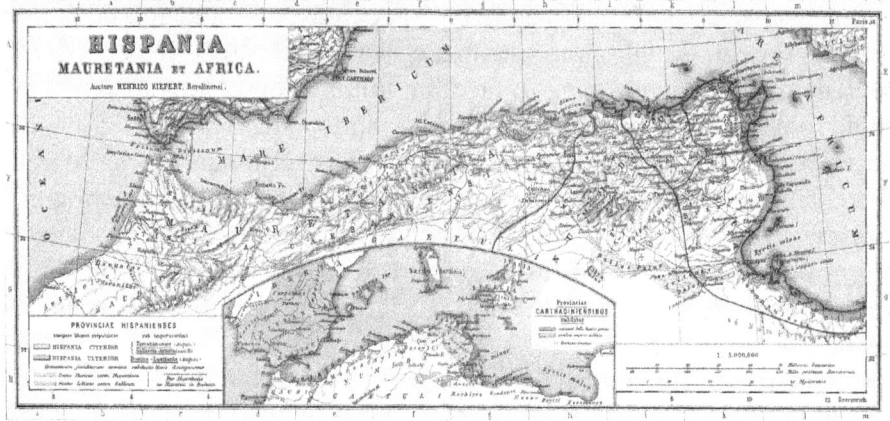

Map containing Mauretania (highlighted in yellow). [87]

It is safe to assume that Mauretania was highly valuable for Rome. Not only was the kingdom's soil well suited to growing olives, which were a staple of the Roman diet, but garum, a type of preserved fish paste beloved by the Romans, was also produced in Mauretania. Other supplies, such as wood, horses, and other exotic animals commonly used by the Romans in the arena, were also exported from the kingdom. Mauretania's wealth, combined with its military and naval strength, allowed the kingdom to prosper in its own right—at least before it got annexed by Rome.

After Augustus made Juba II the new ruler of the kingdom, Mauretania experienced a period of change. Despite his Berber heritage, Juba II planned to embrace Roman culture and spread it across the kingdom. The process of Romanization began in earnest, as Juba II never shied away from promoting Roman architecture, art, and language to the people he ruled.

Since Mauretania was a Roman client kingdom, it witnessed the arrival of Roman officials who were tasked with governing the region. Roman laws and customs were soon introduced to the locals. Juba II even renamed the kingdom's capital, Iol, to Caesarea in honor of Julius Caesar. In just a few years, Roman architecture began to dot the region, from forums to Roman baths and theaters.

Juba II was given the opportunity to rule Mauretania but only to a certain degree. As a client king, he was always under the watchful eye of Rome. Juba II was expected to never ignore Rome's call to arms; he was expected to provide military support to Rome when needed. The empire, which continued to grow each day, needed a lot of supplies, and it was Mauretania's responsibility to meet Rome's needs. Juba was also expected to maintain his kingdom's political stability. Even the smallest signs of unrest had to be dealt with immediately before it turned into chaos and forced Rome to intervene. In return, Juba II and his kingdom could enjoy protection from any external threats.

The tomb of Juba II and his wife, Cleopatra Selene II, in Tipaza, Algeria.[88]

King Juba II was loyal to Augustus, which allowed the kingdom to remain on the empire's good side. However, despite Juba II's successful reign and efforts to Romanize Mauretania, problems emerged. Although the Mauretanian elites were quick to adapt to Roman rule—they even embraced Latin as the official language of administration—the same could not be said about the common people. While Romanization was obvious in the center of the kingdom, Berber traditions and language persisted, especially in the rural areas. The imposition of Roman laws and taxation and the presence of Roman soldiers eventually created tensions. Over time, these tensions grew into revolts.

One of the most memorable revolts that took place against Roman authorities happened when the kingdom was under the reign of Ptolemy of Mauretania (the son of Juba II and his wife, Cleopatra Selene II). Ptolemy was invited to Rome and was said to have arrived in a spectacular fashion. He was dressed lavishly in his royal attire, which might have sparked the jealousy of the Roman emperor, Caligula.

Caligula has been described by historians as extremely erratic and violent, and he ordered Ptolemy's execution shortly after his arrival. His death undoubtedly led Mauretania to fall into political chaos, which eventually led to a major uprising. Led by the chieftain Aedemon (a former slave of Ptolemy), the Mauretanians began to plot on how to reclaim their independence from Roman rule. At first, it seemed as if the Berbers might succeed, especially when the Roman throne was passed to Claudius, whom many thought to be unfit to rule. He was believed to have suffered from a combination of physical and neurological conditions. Unfortunately for the rebels, Claudius proved to be a reliable ruler after all.

The emperor dispatched seasoned Roman generals and legions to Mauretania, where they faced the rebels head-on. Although the Berber forces were fierce and had experience in battles, they were no match for the highly trained and better-equipped Roman legions. The Romans engaged in siege warfare, aiming to subdue fortified strongholds of the Berber tribes throughout Mauretania.

By 44 CE, the rebellion had been suppressed. This allowed Claudius to formally annex the kingdom and separate it into two Roman provinces: Mauretania Tingitana in the west (modern-day Morocco) and Mauretania Caesariensis in the east (modern-day northern Algeria). There were revolts every now and then, but the Romans were able to quell them. The provinces of Mauretania Tingitana and Mauretania Caesariensis remained a part of the empire until the arrival of the Vandals in 429 CE and the collapse of Roman authority in the region.

Chapter 8 – Forgotten Empires of Late Antiquity: Axum and Djenné-Djenno

The world is vast, and every inch is filled with countless stories of different civilizations. Africa is a massive continent. Yet, the spotlight rarely reaches all of the land. While history often highlights ancient civilizations like the Greeks, the Romans, the Egyptians, and the Chinese, others—despite being equally remarkable—tend to fade into the background. These so-called "forgotten empires" played important roles in shaping ancient trade, culture, and governance. However, they are often left in obscurity, usually not intentionally but due to their remote locations and the lack of written records and artifacts.

In recent decades, there has been renewed interest in Africa's ancient past, especially as historians and archaeologists successfully uncover more sites, relics, and artifacts. These pieces of the puzzle allow professionals to reconstruct the stories of these forgotten empires, bringing their achievements and way of life back into the light. Through these findings, we can get a clearer picture of Africa's ancient past, revealing civilizations that traded, innovated, and governed with sophistication equal to their more widely known counterparts.

The Axumite Empire, the First Sub-Saharan African State to Embrace Christianity

Axum was located in northeastern Africa (in a region called Tigray) where the Ethiopian Highlands met the Red Sea. Due to its strategic location, bridging the continents of Africa, Asia, and Europe, Axum was seen as a hub of commerce. Of course, everything has a beginning, but scholars were still debating Axum's mysterious origins.

The Kingdom of Axum at its height.[89]

Humans have lived in the region where the Axumite Empire would soon form since the Stone Age. However, the exact beginnings and origins of Axum are still unclear. Scholars suggest that people from the Kingdom of Saba, located across the Red Sea in what is now Yemen, might have migrated into the area around the 1st millennium BCE and influenced local culture. Archaeologists have also uncovered evidence of an earlier society known as Di'amat (also known as D'MT or D'mt) in the region. The kingdom centered around the village of Yeha, about fifty kilometers northeast of where Axum would emerge.

Interestingly, this kingdom was not the only one to have existed near the site of Axum; there seems to have been another city-state that thrived on Bieta Giyorgis Hill, right next to the Axumite Empire, though this hill eventually became part of the empire later on. Although much remains uncertain, for now, it is safe to assume that these early influences and connections likely laid the groundwork for Axum's rise by the 1st century CE.

The key to the kingdom's early success was its control over trade routes across the Red Sea and into the Arabian Peninsula. By securing these routes, Axum was able to link Africa's riches with foreign markets. Its trading partners included most of the major powers in the known world, including South Arabia, Egypt, the Middle East, India, and China. Merchants from these regions flocked to the port of Adulis, where they haggled in a mix of languages, from the Axumites' native tongue, Ge'ez, to Greek, Latin, and Arabic.

While gold and ivory were among Axum's most valuable export items, the kingdom was also well known for the trafficking of frankincense, myrrh, emeralds, salt, tortoise shells, rhinoceros horns, and even enslaved people. Exotic animals, such as lions, cheetahs, and elephants, were also prized exports. These animals often ended up in Roman arenas. Axum's import commodities included olive oil, wine, spices, weapons, glassware, and intricate jewelry. Interestingly, the kingdom was the very first African nation to have minted its own coins. Archaeologists have discovered Axumite coins in sites as far away as India.

Axumite gold coins.[40]

The kingdom owed its success to its formidable military. With the wealth that the kingdom possessed, expansion was inevitable. Multiple campaigns were launched across the Red Sea into Yemen and the Arabian Peninsula with the goal of controlling critical trade routes. The Axumite soldiers were well equipped and well structured. They marched into battles wearing armor made from iron and bronze. It was also common for these soldiers to carry charms with them, as they believed they could give them protection. Religion was embedded deeply into the hearts of the Axumites; campaigns usually began with ceremonial blessings where priests would invoke the gods' favor.

The Axumite kings were skilled in both warfare and diplomacy, and the Axumites succeeded in extending their influence beyond the African continent by the 3rd century CE. According to a few inscribed Axumite stone tablets, the battles in the Arabian Peninsula were fierce. The Axumites were said to have launched several intense sieges and defeated the local chieftains in the region. Their success in expanding their reach into southern Arabia undoubtedly solidified Axum's reputation. Word of its might traveled far beyond the continent, reaching even the Romans. Upon their return to the capital city, the military would be welcomed with grand celebrations, with the people performing songs and dances and holding feasts to honor their bravery.

Back in the highlands, the common people lived an equally vibrant life, although it was simpler. The Axumites were experts in agriculture, so scenes of farmers cultivating wheat, barley, and teff in terraced fields were common sights. Their daily lives revolved around the seasons. Families typically worked together. While men toiled in the fields and spent hours striking the anvil, Axumite women had their own responsibilities. They mainly managed the household and weaved textiles, which were then sold in the bustling marketplaces. When it was time to celebrate their bountiful harvest, the Axumites held feasts and rituals dedicated to their gods, particularly Mahrem.

Religion was one of the most important aspects of being an Axumite. They worshiped a pantheon of gods, with Mahrem being the chief of all deities. The god was also believed to be the father of Axumite kings. Temples, typically built of carved stone, once housed idols and altars used for rituals. The best-known architectural wonders of Axum are the towering stelae, which can be found today at the Northern Stelae Field (located at the archaeological site of Axum).

The stele dedicated to King Remhai stood tallest; it measured about thirty-three meters tall. Underneath it, one could also find a twelve-room tomb, with one of the rooms containing none other than the sealed coffin of Remhai himself. Despite being one of the most impressive monuments in the region—it featured thirteen exquisitely carved granite blocks—the stele, unfortunately, crumbled to the ground shortly after being erected in the 3rd century CE. Its remnants can still be seen today.

The Axumite stele lying on the ground where it crumbled.⁴¹

King Ezana's Stele, on the other hand, stands today at twenty-three meters. Considered to be one of the most well-preserved stelae in Axum, this structure was constructed to commemorate King Ezana himself. The obelisk is adorned with decorative "windows" and "doors," mimicking a multi-storied building. Scholars suggest that this design was to symbolize the royal palaces the king had built during his reign.

Today, the title of the tallest and most famous Axumite stele goes to the Obelisk of Axum. This structure, however, was actually looted by Italian forces in 1937—a time when Ethiopia was occupied by Italy. The stele, which stood at about twenty-four meters tall, was transported to Rome and erected in the Piazza di Porta Capena. It was only after a few decades of successful diplomatic negotiations that Italy agreed to return the stele to where it belonged. In 2008, the structure was reinstalled in its original location, thus restoring a piece of Axum's heritage.

The Obelisk of Axum standing proud in Ethiopia today.[45]

King Ezana Embracing Christianity

In 330 CE, Axum's ruler, King Ezana, made a major decision that would alter the course of both his empire and history. Ezana was known to be a skilled, insightful, and, at times, kind ruler. He conquered many lands, but the king was known to have acted differently than other victorious rulers, especially to the people he conquered. Instead of oppressing or enslaving them, the king moved them to fertile land where they were able to live normal lives. They were able to cultivate, make money off the land, and contribute to the kingdom. This move to see conquered people prosper rather than suffer was rare during the time.

However, the king's acts of kindness were not the only things that contributed to his name being immortalized in history books. King Ezana chose to embrace Christianity in the 4th century CE, becoming the first Axumite king to adopt the faith as his kingdom's official religion. Of course, the king did not make this decision hastily. In fact, his conversion came as a result of exposure to Christian teachings by the Phoenician Christian missionary Frumentius and his brother, Aedesius.

Frumentius's arrival in the Kingdom of Axum was not welcomed at first. His crew was massacred by the locals, and the brothers were taken as captives by the reigning Axumite king, Ousanas (Ezana's father). However, the two eventually gained favor from the king. Later, Frumentius and Aedesius were given the responsibility of tutoring Ezana.

Known for his openness to new ideas, King Ezana found significance in these teachings and, after years of reflection, declared Christianity the official faith of Axum. The new religion infused new meaning into Axumite life. Priests were made community leaders, and their tasks included offering guidance to those in need and interpreting the Christian scriptures.

The empire also saw the emergence of new churches and monasteries. King Ezana commissioned one sometime in the 4th century CE. Known as the Church of Our Lady Mary of Zion, the church was not only the oldest of Ethiopia's churches but was also believed to have been the very location where the Ark of the Covenant was preserved. The cathedral witnessed a few episodes of destruction—the most significant one occurred during the invasion of the Islamic leader Ahmed Gregn—yet each time, it was rebuilt.

The Church of Our Lady Mary Zion today.[48]

It is safe to say that the impact of Christianity reached beyond spiritual life. The empire's Christian identity reshaped Axum's connections with the outside world. Its alliances with other Christian states across the Red Sea and into the Mediterranean were greatly strengthened. Byzantine envoys visited Axum, exchanging ideas and religious thoughts with the locals. For years, Axum thrived as a center of trade, culture, and faith—at least until the later years of antiquity.

The Lost City of Djenné-Djenno

For centuries, the Niger River has served as a lifeline for travelers, traders, and settlers alike. It flows like a life-giving artery through the vast landscapes of West Africa, providing both sustenance and a path for trade. Its winding course carves through Mali and nourishes the lands along its banks. It was also in this region that a city emerged.

Known as Djenné-Djenno, the city is Africa's oldest urban center. Its roots can be traced back to around 250 BCE. When Djenné-Djenno reached its golden age, the city was thought to have looked like a dream. Those who arrived by either the river or on camelback were welcomed by the sights of bustling markets, the sounds of merchants haggling in different languages and dialects filling the air. While potters were busy shaping clay, crafting their next work of art, children could be seen running along the streets, their laughter bringing the city to life. Mudbrick homes dotted the city, and towering granaries were built among the palm trees.

Given its location along the Niger River, the people of Djenné-Djenno were blessed with fertile soil and abundant water resources. Early settlers knew the precious value of their land, and the people of Djenné-Djenno made agriculture their lifeblood. Crops like rice, millet, and sorghum flourished in the floodplains surrounding the city, where they enjoyed predictable floods and summer rains. The people also domesticated animals such as cows, goats, and sheep. It is safe to say that this agricultural abundance did not only sustain the local population. It also allowed Djenné-Djenno to eventually transform itself from a mere settlement into a major trading hub, attracting various civilizations across West Africa and beyond.

By the end of the 3rd century CE, the city's traders began importing stones, which they turned into grindstones. Iron ore and copper were brought into the city for metalworking. Using iron-smelting techniques, blacksmiths were able to create more advanced tools and weapons.

When the city entered the 6th century CE, its pottery became popular and was exported to different parts of the world.

The city of Djenné-Djenno was best known for its urban design. Many other ancient cities had their infrastructure organized around a central palace or a certain religious structure. Egyptians, for instance, tended to build their cities centered around their main temples. The people of Djenné-Djenno, however, built their city differently. Their city was made up of nearly forty distinct mounds spread across a four-kilometer area.

However, these mounds were not natural hills. Instead, they were elevated layers formed over time as homes and structures were built, lived in, abandoned, and rebuilt again in the same spot. Each mound possibly housed a specific social group. It could be plausible that they were organized by family ties, occupation, or shared responsibility. These "corporate communities," as scholars call them, typically operated as tightly knit units within the large city. Although Djenné-Djenno was decentralized, it was still a well-organized urban center.

Each mound had dozens of houses and public buildings made of mudbrick, which offered natural insulation against the harsh sun. The majority of these buildings had flat roofs, which served as additional spaces for living or work activities. This architectural style was the precursor to later, more popular structures in present-day Mali, especially the famous Great Mosque of Djenné.

Granaries were raised on stilts to keep their goods from being infested with pests. Since the mounds were disjointed, each group had its own trade expertise, like pottery, blacksmithing, or farming. This way, the city was able to thrive without strict hierarchies. Each community supplied goods and services to one another, creating a system of interdependence that kept the economy steady and diversified.

The nucleus of the city was, of course, its marketplace. With the ancient city's strategic location along the Niger River and its connections to the trade routes across the Sahara, Djenné-Djenno was economically successful. Every hour of the day, merchants and their caravans would travel through the area, bringing all sorts of valuable goods from different parts of the world into the buzzing markets of Djenné-Djenno. Hundreds of boats laden with goods docked at the city's harbor, creating a constant flow of resources that further fueled the city's growth.

Some of the key items commonly traded in the city included gold, ivory, spices, pottery, and jewelry. Kola nuts were also highly valued in the marketplace. They were typically chewed for their stimulating effects, as they provided a burst of energy. Apart from its stimulating properties, this caffeine-containing nut also held significant cultural and religious value. In West African cultures, people would chew it at social gatherings like weddings and funerals. The Igbo of Nigeria used kola nuts in sacred offerings and prayers to their ancestors.

Kola nuts spread out and ready for sale."

Although no concrete evidence has been uncovered, scholars suggest that the people of Djenné-Djenno were deeply spiritual. Similar to other West African societies of the time, those from Djenné-Djenno likely had beliefs rooted in natural spirits and ancestors. Archaeological discoveries of shrines and altars within homes and courtyards seem to support this claim. Food, various crafted items, or perhaps small figurines were placed at these shrines. It is likely the people performed many different ceremonies and rituals.

The name Djenné-Djenno is unfamiliar to many. For centuries, the city's remains were hidden under layers of soil and plants, its secrets and stories sealed from humanity. It was only when archaeologists began to uncover its ruins in the 20th century that the city began to receive the spotlight it deserved. Through multiple series of excavations, archaeologists succeeded in retrieving artifacts, such as terracotta sculptures, pottery, and even remnants of buildings. After finding these items, scholars were able to provide insights into the lives of those who once lived in the city.

The terracotta sculptures captured the attention of many. These detailed sculptures came in many forms, from humans to animals, each with exaggerated features and unique postures. Sculptures representing warriors or perhaps hunters feature muscular limbs and have fierce expressions on their faces. Animal sculptures typically have elongated necks or stylized bodies, which possibly indicate they were from local mythology or served as totems.

A terracotta sculpture from Djenné-Djenno covered with red ochre."

However, by the end of the 1st millennium CE, Djenné-Djenno began to witness its influence waning. This was mostly due to the emergence of new trade routes and the rise of other cities along the Niger River. Combined with possible environmental changes, these shifts in the trans-Saharan trade network eventually drew people and resources away from Djenné-Djenno, as merchants became more attracted to the riches of other cities. The rise of political centers within the Mali Empire also likely contributed to its decline.

Chapter 9 – Enigmatic Ruins and Mythical Cities of Ancient Africa

Nabta Playa, the Oldest Astronomical Observatory on Earth

Nabta Playa is known as the oldest astronomical observatory on earth, with its roots traced back to about seven thousand years ago. Located in the heart of the Nubian Desert in southern Egypt—not far from the Sudanese border—some might even refer to it as Africa's Stonehenge, although the site is far older than its British counterpart.

From afar, Nabta Playa may seem like an ordinary archaeological site. The ground consists of a cluster of stone circles, lines, and slabs. However, these stones and slabs were placed there for a reason. The ancient people who once inhabited the region used Nabta Playa for astronomical reasons.

A reconstruction of Nabta Playa.⁴⁶

Similar to many other archaeological sites, these megaliths were abandoned and forgotten as time passed. The story of how these ancient megaliths is interesting. A Bedouin (nomadic Arab) named Eide Mariff stumbled upon the stones while crossing the Sahara in the 1970s. Surprised to see such a peculiar site in the middle of the barren desert, Mastiff decided to take his colleague, the American archaeologist Fred Wendorf, to the site. Wendorf's longtime friend and collaborator, Romuald Schild, told this story differently. He claimed that he and Wendorf came across the megaliths themselves as they drove across the desert. Regardless, it was from this point on that Nabta Playa began to receive the world's attention.

Archaeologists and scholars deduced that these stones were arranged to align with the summer solstice. The stones essentially acted as a calendar and helped the people anticipate seasonal changes, such as the arrival of monsoon rains. Through this understanding of astronomy, the inhabitants of Nabta Playa were able to plan agricultural and social activities around the cycles of nature. The site is also thought to have served as a place where rituals and social gatherings took place. Various objects have been found at Nabta Playa, including animal bones, clay vessels, and even remnants of huts, all of which suggest that inhabitants convened here regularly.

Jebel Barkal

Jebel Barkal.[47]

Jebel Barkal overlooks the Nile in southern Sudan. This modestly sized sandstone mountain may seem unremarkable at first glance, but it was once a sacred place to the ancient Kushites and Egyptians. To them, this was where heaven touched Earth and the very location where gods walked among mortals. Sometimes referred to as the "Pure Mountain," Jebel Barkal was believed to be the residence of none other than Amun, the most important deity in the Egyptian and Kushite pantheons.

What remains of Jebel Barkal today are only dusty ruins, but over three thousand years ago, the site was home to multiple grand temples. There were about thirteen in total. When the area was conquered by Pharaoh Thutmose III in 1450 BCE, Jebel Barkal was turned into a fortified settlement that marked the southern limit of the Egyptian kingdom. Under the reigns of the Egyptian pharaohs, Jebel Barkal saw the emergence of grand temples, which were constructed to honor the ancient gods. The Temple of Mut and the Temple of Amun were seen as the most sacred and important of all.

When Kushite kings rose to power, they still saw Jebel Barkal as an important site. In fact, it became the spiritual epicenter of their flourishing empire. New temples were constructed, and the old ones went through expansion projects. The mountain was where Kushite pharaohs claimed legitimacy as god-appointed rulers of both Kush and Egypt.

Perhaps one of the most interesting features of the mountain is its natural pinnacle on the summit, which resembles a cobra. Since a cobra was a powerful symbol in both Egyptian and Kushite iconography—it represented royalty and protection—it is safe to assume that ancient worshipers viewed the mountain as a divine sign that their gods were the ones who fashioned the mountain so that it could watch over their chosen people.

Tassili n'Ajjer

Tassili n'Ajjer is a sandstone plateau in southeastern Algeria. Unfolding like a vast canvas in the

The ruins of the Temple of Amun at Jebel Barkal.[48]

middle of the Sahara, this historical location features a maze of rock formations and hidden valleys. The most important aspect of Tassili n'Ajjer, however, is the astonishing collection of prehistoric art. Handpainted by the area's inhabitants thousands of years ago, this rock art collection is now considered one of the largest and most significant in the African continent.

The area stretches over seventy-two thousand square kilometers, and there are over fifteen thousand petroglyphs and paintings. Some of them date back as early as twelve thousand years ago. Most of these paintings pictured scenes of a lush and green Sahara—a depiction that may seem rather mythical by today's standards. According to these rock paintings, the Sahara once teemed with life; rivers flowed, trees grew throughout the land, and a myriad of animals roamed around freely.

An aerial view of Tassili n'Ajjer.[49]

Of course, the art style of these paintings evolved as time went by. The earliest paintings often feature ghostly human figures with rounded, mask-like heads. They were usually depicted participating in rituals and dances. Later art shows more realistic portrayals. The most common images of this time were pastoral scenes of cattle herding and hunting, perhaps suggesting that with climate change, the people transitioned from hunter-gatherers to herders.

A colorful rock painting from Tassili n'Ajjer depicting cattle herding.[50]

Apart from insights into the lifestyles of the inhabitants back then, the images found in Tassili n'Ajjer also offer a glimpse into the spiritual and communal lives of early Saharan societies. There are paintings of supernatural-looking beings that might have been ancient deities or spirits. The exact meaning of these paintings remains a mystery, but it is hard to dismiss that Tassili n'Ajjer is a site that shows the rich cultural scene of early Africa. Each of its winding passages and rock art silently narrates stories of a lost world. This location is so important that it has been named a UNESCO World Heritage Site.

Tellem

The Tellem were an ancient people who dwelled in what is now Mali. They are mostly known today for their impressive cliffside settlement along the Bandiagara Escarpment. Their cliff dwellings were typically carved into sheer rock faces hundreds of feet above the valley floor. Their settlement included windowless dwellings and a series of other structures vital for a community, such as granaries and burial sites, all of which were embedded directly into the cliffs.

The settlement dates back to around the 11th century CE. Accessing the settlement was not an easy task, especially for outsiders. One must go through a steep, narrow, and perilous path before they could enter the settlement. These cliff dwellings served practical purposes. Apart from protecting the community from potential invaders, its location above the valley ensured their food supplies were spared from seasonal floods.

Archaeologists have unearthed different artifacts left by the Tellem. Pottery, carved figurines, and woven textiles were found, which provided some insights into their cultural life. Ritual objects were also uncovered, many of which suggest that the Tellem practiced a form of ancestor worship or animism. Their woven textiles were rather vibrant and showed that their advanced weaving techniques were sophisticated for their time.

The cliff dwellings of the Tellem people.[61]

However, by the 15th century CE, the Tellem disappeared. Their cliffside villages were abandoned. Scholars claim this had something to do with climate change. After finding it hard to survive on the cliffs, the people might have left to join other thriving communities. Another theory suggests they might have been forced out of their villages by invading communities. Regardless, their legacy lived on. The region was inhabited by the Dogon people, who preserved some of the Tellem people's traditions.

Gedi

Gedi (also spelled as Gede) is an ancient town that stood within dense forests along Kenya's coast. Hidden away near the Indian Ocean, this town has been recognized by some as one of Africa's most mystifying ruins due to its unclear fate. From what remains of the town, including the stone walls, mosques, palaces, and homes, scholars are able to conclude that this was the location where a Swahili settlement once thrived. Existing as early as the 13th century, Gedi was thought to have experienced a golden age in the 16th century. It was once a highly organized town with impressive architecture, but mentions of it in historical records are scarce, leading to its story being shrouded in complete mystery.

What remains of Gedi.⁵³

Although the ruins of the town are now surrounded by towering baobabs and strangler figs, making the site look like a forgotten city from a bedtime story, back in its heyday, Gedi was a cosmopolitan center of trade and culture. Archaeologists have unearthed various goods, including Chinese porcelain, Venetian glass, and even Persian pottery. This indicates that the town was part of a far-reaching trade network that connected Africa with Asia, the Mediterranean, and the Middle East. Its inhabitants, possibly the Swahili people, were experts in trade, agriculture, and craftsmanship. The town had a rather sophisticated urban design. Stone buildings filled the landscape, with most featuring arched doorways and decorative carvings. Gedi also had drainage systems, which were uncommon in much of sub-Saharan Africa at the time.

However, Gedi was mysteriously abandoned by the early 17th century. While some suggest this happened due to the Portuguese expansion along the coast, which disrupted local trade routes, others argued that the town's abandonment was largely due to shifts in water resources or perhaps an outbreak of disease. Another theory is that the inhabitants might have left their once-thriving town to save themselves from hostile tribes nearby. Of course, none of these theories have been confirmed to be true since no definitive evidence that explains their sudden departure has been found. No written records have ever been found; the only thing the people of Gedi left behind was the remnants of their town, with its ghostly structures gradually claimed by Mother Nature, who perhaps intended to conceal Gedi's secrets.

Sabratha and Leptis Magna, Two of the Most Impressive Roman Cities

Sabratha and Leptis Magna were two impressive ancient cities perched along the coast of present-day Libya. These cities flourished under Roman rule. Before they were abandoned, both Sabratha and Leptis Magna were believed to appear so sophisticated that many suggested divine or otherworldly forces inspired their design. From colossal temples to grand amphitheaters, these ruins remain breathtaking even in their abandoned state.

The theater of Sabratha.[58]

Overlooking the Mediterranean, Sabratha is believed to trace back to the Phoenician era. The remnants of statues of gods and goddesses, as well as the intricacy of the temple ruins, suggest that the city might have been spiritually significant. These were not the only objects uncovered in the city; inscriptions in Latin, Greek, and even the Punic script were left by ancient people, offering us a tiny window into the city's cosmopolitan character.

However, the most iconic structure of the grand city is, of course, the theater of Sabratha. This architectural marvel features stone seating that could host thousands of people at a time. Its stage featured an intricate backdrop. The row of columns made the theater extravagant, and its dozens of bas-reliefs depicting various scenes and characters, both mythological and historical, added to the theater's beauty.

The ruins of Leptis Magna."

Farther east, one can find Leptis Magna. This city reached its golden age under the reign of Emperor Septimius Severus, who was born in North Africa. Similar to Sabratha, Leptis Magna had its own iconic structures. One of them is the arch dedicated to the emperor, known simply today as the Arch of Septimius Severus. The city also boasted a vast marketplace and a basilica adorned with detailed carvings.

The Arch of Septimius Severus in Leptis Magna. [55]

Pliny the Elder once described the divine beauty of these cities in his writings. According to the ancient writer, at their height, these cities seemed to be realms beyond human making. The lines of columns, exquisite carvings, and the sprawling marketplaces gave the cities an otherworldly aura. Some might even describe them as being touched by the gods themselves.

Wagadu, the City That Got Destroyed by a Man's Defiance

Mythical cities have long captivated human imagination. From the submerged city of Atlantis to the golden riches of El Dorado, these lost places often evoke a sense of wonder, tempting explorers to search for the hidden truths in the stories about them. When it comes to mythical locations, these places are often symbols of something greater or rather divine. These were typically places where gods walked, heroes ruled, and knowledge beyond mortal understanding was hidden. While the lost city of Atlantis is the example that often comes to mind whenever we think of mythical cities, it is far from the only one. The Lost City of Z is believed to be hidden somewhere in the Amazon, and the Himalayas is supposedly home to the riches of Shambhala. But believe it or not, Africa is also home to an array of equally intriguing mythical cities, each complete with its own sets of mysteries and secrets. One great example is a city named Wagadu.

The Soninke people are one of the oldest ethnic groups in West Africa. They are best known as the founders of the ancient Ghana Empire. Being masters of trade, agriculture, and governance, the Soninke managed to establish a powerful society that thrived from the 4th century to the 13th century CE. Located in what is now southeastern Mauritania and Mali, their prosperous economy depended heavily on the trade of gold, salt, and other resources. However, apart from their wealth and massive influence in West Africa, the Soninke had a rich oral tradition, which included legends and moral lessons. One of the most intriguing fables that came from the Soninke was the tale of Wagadu, a legendary city that is thought to have been associated with the Empire of Ghana.

According to this legend, Wagadu held immense wealth. Gold flowed through its gates freely, and prosperity never left its inhabitants. Its downfall happened when the city failed to meet the demand of a certain deity. Known as Bida, this mystical serpent deity lived in Wagadu and was worshiped by the inhabitants of the city. The deity was the one responsible for the city's never-ending wealth. However, in exchange for this prosperity, the people of Wagadu had to offer Bida a sacrifice in the form of a young maiden every year. By meeting this demand, Wagadu would be blessed with a continuous flow of gold and resources, and Bida would protect the city from all harm.

The tale took a dramatic turn with a certain young man named Mamadi. His fiancée, who went by the name Sia, was the one chosen by the people of Wagadu to be the next sacrifice for Bida. Refusing to let go of his lover, Mamadi went against the priests and fought an entire army sent by the king. He wanted to save his fiancée from her fate, so he went into the forest where Bida lived. Hiding behind a tree, he waited for Bida to emerge before slashing off the serpent deity's head. He did this multiple times since Bida's head kept growing back after each slash. It took Mamadi seven attempts until Bida finally lay lifeless on the ground.

While Mamadi managed to escape Wagadu with his fiancée, the city eventually met its end. Without Bida's divine powers, drought took over the land, killing all the animals and crops that sustained the people. This catastrophe led to the destruction of the city, and those who survived became nomads.

The Lost City of the Kalahari

Many believe the Lost City of the Kalahari lay deep within the sprawling Kalahari Desert. Legends of this city's existence reached a larger audience in the late 19th century when the Canadian explorer and funambulist William Leonard Hunt (better known by his stage name, Guillermo Farini) claimed to have stumbled across stone ruins as he traversed the desert. According to Farini, he saw parts of stone walls and a few other structures protruding from the desert sands. This sight led him to believe that he had discovered the remains of an ancient city. He documented his findings in an account called *Through the Kalahari Desert*, which sparked curiosity and speculation among many adventurers and archaeologists.

Unfortunately, Farini's descriptions were rather vague. Despite no concrete evidence of such a city, his account led to numerous expeditions in search of the fabled city. Some embarked on the journey to find the city driven by the motivation—or belief—that the lost city might contain riches and historical treasures. As time passed by, more theories emerged, with some suggesting that it could have been an outpost of a forgotten culture, possibly influenced by Phoenician, Egyptian, or even pre-colonial African civilizations. There are also those who speculate that the Lost City of the Kalahari could be connected to the Great Zimbabwe ruins or any other stone-building culture of ancient Africa.

Of course, there are many skeptics who argue the existence of the city. Instead of remnants of an ancient city, they claim what Farini saw was natural rock formations shaped by erosion. After all, the Kalahari Desert is known for its unique geological features, so Farini could have been mistaken. Expeditions continued throughout the 20th century, yet no definitive proof of the city has ever been found. While some believe the city's existence to be completely fictional or exaggerated, there are others who still hold out hope that one day, the remnants of this ancient city will appear.

Conclusion

Africa's ancient past holds far more than meets the eye. Oftentimes, our understanding of the continent's history is filtered through a limited lens, with Egypt and a few other well-known empires taking over the narrative. It is safe to say that Africa's history is as complex as other parts of the world. Its story extends beyond the Nile to include not only prehistoric tribes and thriving trading hubs that shaped the continent and also the wider world but also forgotten kingdoms and powerful empires, many of which were misunderstood or even villainized in Western accounts. The mysteries of Punt, the advanced metal technologies of the Nok, the resilience of the Saharan tribes, and the rise of bigger empires like Carthage and Kush are just some of the examples that reveal a side of Africa that defies traditional perspectives.

The message in this book is clear: Africa was never an isolated land. Rather, it was a colorful continent full of stories, legends, and mysteries that rival those in other parts of the world. The various civilizations that once called this land home have carved distinct identities through their art, language, spiritual practices, and technological achievements. From the busy trade centers of Carthage, where merchants exchanged an array of goods from across the Mediterranean, to the rise of the kingdoms of Numidia and Mauretania, whose skilled warriors made them both allies and rivals of Rome, each society left its own mark on history.

Another common misperception of ancient Africa is that it was isolated from the larger world. Yet, the truth is completely the opposite. African empires were connected by vast networks that linked them with major parts of the world, from Europe to the Middle East. The Kingdom of Axum was known to have traded across the Red Sea, with evidence proving it interacted with distant powers. The continent was also home to many innovations. Take the Garamantes, for example, who created complex irrigation systems, allowing them to cultivate crops in the unforgiving Sahara Desert. Ancient Africans were not merely surviving. They were thriving and influencing the broader world.

Indeed, Africa's ancient history is filled with achievements, many of which could be placed on par with any other civilizations beyond the continent. Grand architecture, advanced metalworking and craftsmanship, complex social systems, and bustling trade networks all flourished across its vast landscapes. However, if only one word could be used to describe the African people, then resilience might be the best one.

The ancient African people went through a lot—shifting climates, migrations, and interactions, both peaceful and hostile, with outside empires—yet they never refrained from demonstrating remarkable adaptability. The Kingdom of Nubia is one of the best examples. It prospered at the same time as ancient Egypt, and Nubia was undoubtedly heavily influenced by Egyptian culture. Yet, the Nubians did not simply copy their neighbor's practices; they adapted and modified the Egyptian culture to fit their own unique environment, values, and cultural identity.

Africa's societies found ways to make their land their home. Their story teaches us that resilience is not just about survival. It is also about living in harmony with the land, preserving wisdom, and leaving behind footprints that inspire us even today.

Here's another book by Matt Clayton that you might like

Free Bonus from Captivating History (Available for a Limited time)

Hi History Lovers!

Now you have a chance to join our exclusive history list so you can get your first history ebook for free as well as discounts and a potential to get more history books for free!

Simply visit the link below to join.

Or, Scan the QR code!

captivatinghistory.com/ebook

Also, make sure to follow us on Facebook, X, and YouTube by searching for Captivating History.

Bibliography

Badian, E. "Syphax | Numidian Ruler, Punic War Leader." *Encyclopedia Britannica*. July 20, 1998. www.britannica.com/biography/Syphax.

Betz, Eric. "Nabta Playa: The World's First Astronomical Site Was Built in Africa and Is Older Than Stonehenge." *Astronomy Magazine*. May 18, 2023. www.astronomy.com/observing/nabta-playa-the-worlds-first-astronomical-site-was-built-in-africa-and-is-older-than-stonehenge.

Cartwright, Mark. "Carthaginian Government." *World History Encyclopedia*. June 15, 2016. www.worldhistory.org/Carthaginian_Government.

Cartwright, Mark. "Carthaginian Trade." *World History Encyclopedia*. June 17, 2016. www.worldhistory.org/article/911/carthaginian-trade.

Dhwty. "Gods of Carthage and the Punic Power House of Baal Hammon and Tanit." *Ancient Origins*. June 13, 2019, www.ancient-origins.net/ancient-places-africa/baal-hammon-and-tanit-0012136.

El-Diwany, Tarek. "Somalia: The Ancient Lost Kingdom of Punt Is Finally Found?" *Ancient Origins*. Apr 18, 2019. www.ancient-origins.net/ancient-places-africa/somalia-ancient-lost-kingdom-punt-finally-found-006893.

"Ezana of Axum: The King of Kindness." *Our Ancestories*. Jan 30, 2021, our-ancestories.com/blogs/news/ezana-of-axum-the-king-of-kindness?srsltid=AfmBOooRuFgG5jVcXEPL48LNchYdtapdp-jtnow_pnZLzUp658gEv9ei.

French Press Agency - AFP. "After Decade of Chaos Libya's Roman Jewel City Lies in Limbo." *Daily Sabah*, Sept 26, 2021. www.dailysabah.com/arts/after-decade-of-chaos-libyas-roman-jewel-city-lies-in-limbo/news.

Gillan, Joanna. "The Highly Advanced and Mysterious Ancient Civilization of the Nok." *Ancient Origins*, March 5, 2023. www.ancient-origins.net/ancient-places-africa/highly-advanced-and-mysterious-ancient-civilization-nok-00679#google_vignette.

Gyrus. "The San & The Eland" *Dreamflesh*. 1998. dreamflesh.com/essay/san-eland.

King, Arienne. "Mauretania." *World History Encyclopedia*, May 25, 2023. www.worldhistory.org/Mauretania/#google_vignette.

Mark, Joshua J. "Carthage." *World History Encyclopedia*, May 29, 2020. www.worldhistory.org/carthage.

Mark, Joshua J. "The Kingdom of Kush." *World History Encyclopedia*, Feb 26, 2018, www.worldhistory.org/Kush.

Mark, Joshua J. "The Masaesyli and Massylii of Numidia." *World History Encyclopedia*, Feb 27, 2018. www.worldhistory.org/article/1196/the-masaesyli-and-massylii-of-numidia.

Meddings, Alexander. "Messalina – the Empress Who Remarried While the Emperor Was Out of Town." *Walks Inside Rome*, accessed Oct 20, 2024. www.walksinsiderome.com/blog/messalina-the-empress-who-remarried-while-the-emperor-was-out-of-town/?fbclid=IwZXh0bgNhZW0CMTEAAR2RcEUXpymZEx-Wgv9p6eJfTjRs1YWFXAmQeVdfAmW5sypsqsI3wKnL7to_aem_COQPsea OLhN_AwEFHhuoyQ.

Milligan, Mark. "Kerma – the Ancient African Kingdom." *HeritageDaily - Archaeology News*, Nov 16, 2020. www.heritagedaily.com/2020/11/kerma-the-ancient-african-kingdom/136144.

Milligan, Mark. "Meroë – the Capital of the Kingdom of Kush." *HeritageDaily - Archaeology News*, June 7, 2020. www.heritagedaily.com/2020/06/meroe-the-capital-of-the-kingdom-of-kush/131329.

Metcalfe, Tom. "Nabta Playa: A Mysterious Stone Circle That May Be the World's Oldest Astronomical Observatory." *livescience.com*, Oct 7, 2024. www.livescience.com/archaeology/nabta-playa-a-mysterious-stone-circle-that-may-be-the-worlds-oldest-astronomical-observatory.

"Phoenicians & Hanno the Navigator." *Ages of Exploration*, accessed Nov 4 2024. exploration.marinersmuseum.org/subject/phoenicians-hanno-the-navigator.

"Pierre-François-Xavier Bouchard." *The Linda Hall Library*, Apr 29, 2020. www.lindahall.org/about/news/scientist-of-the-day/pierre-francois-xavier-bouchard.

"Ta Seti, Africa's Early Powerhouse." *Drums of Atlantis*, Aug 11, 2024. drumsofatlantis.com/ta-seti-africas-early-powerhouse.

"Ta-Seti Existed Before Egypt." *On the Shoulders of Giants*, Nov 6, 2024. www.ontheshoulders1.com/the-giants/ta-seti-existed-before-egypt#.

"Ta-Seti, Worlds Oldest Civilization." *Our Weekly*, June 19, 2009. www.ourweekly.com/2009/06/19/ta-seti-worlds-oldest-civilization.

"The Kingdom of Aksum." *National Geographic,* accessed Oct 17, 2024. education.nationalgeographic.org/resource/kingdom-aksum.

"The Sacred Mountain of Jebel Barkal and Ancient Napata." *Kanaga Africa Tours,* accessed Oct 30, 2024. www.kanaga-at.com/en/trip-info/sudan-en/the-sacred-mountain-of-jebel-barkal-and-ancient-napata.

"The Nok Culture." *National Geographic,* accessed Oct 18, 2024. education.nationalgeographic.org/resource/nok-culture.

Tosh, Alistair. "Black Horsemen: Numidian Light Cavalry." *Aspects of History,* accessed Nov 12, 2024. aspectsofhistory.com/black-horsemen-numidian-light-cavalry.

Vučković, Aleksa. "The Great Berber Kingdom of Numidia in the Shadow of Rome." *Ancient Origins,* Jan 20, 2021. www.ancient-origins.net/ancient-places-africa/numidia-0014821.

Image Sources

1. https://commons.wikimedia.org/wiki/File:Vallee_fertile_du_Nil_a_Louxor.jpg#file
2. Roland Unger, CC BY-SA 3.0 <https://creativecommons.org/licenses/by-sa/3.0>, via Wikimedia Commons: https://commons.wikimedia.org/wiki/File:EsnaTempleExample2.jpg
3. Lassi, CC BY-SA 4.0 <https://creativecommons.org/licenses/by-sa/4.0>, via Wikimedia Commons: https://commons.wikimedia.org/wiki/File:Kerma_city.JPG
4. https://elon.io/learn-world-history-1/lesson/9.3.1-the-origin-and-rise-of-the-kingdom-of-kush
5. Walter Callens, CC BY 2.0 <https://creativecommons.org/licenses/by/2.0>, via Wikimedia Commons: https://commons.wikimedia.org/wiki/File:Western_Deffufa_-_Kerma.jpg
6. Matthias Gehricke, CC BY-SA 4.0 <https://creativecommons.org/licenses/by-sa/4.0>, via Wikimedia Commons: https://commons.wikimedia.org/wiki/File:Rulers_of_Kush,_Kerma_Museum.jpg
7. Sue Fleckney, CC BY-SA 2.0 <https://creativecommons.org/licenses/by-sa/2.0>, via Wikimedia Commons: https://commons.wikimedia.org/wiki/File:Taharqo%27s_pyramid,_Nuri,_Sudan,_North-east_Africa.jpg
8. Talessman at en.wikipedia, CC BY 3.0 <https://creativecommons.org/licenses/by/3.0>, via Wikimedia Commons: https://commons.wikimedia.org/wiki/File:NE_200bc.jpg
9. Ron Van Oers, CC BY-SA 3.0 IGO <https://creativecommons.org/licenses/by-sa/3.0/igo/deed.en>, via Wikimedia Commons: https://commons.wikimedia.org/wiki/File:Archaeological_Sites_of_the_Island_of_Meroe-114973.jpg

10 Louvre Museum, CC BY-SA 3.0 <http://creativecommons.org/licenses/by-sa/3.0/>, via Wikimedia Commons: https://commons.wikimedia.org/wiki/File:Minnakht_01.JPG

11 Hans Hillewaert. This file is licensed under the Creative Commons Attribution-Share Alike 4.0 International license: https://commons.wikimedia.org/wiki/File:Rosetta_Stone.JPG

12 Σταύρος, CC BY 2.0 <https://creativecommons.org/licenses/by/2.0>, via Wikimedia Commons: https://commons.wikimedia.org/wiki/File:Relief_of_Hatshepsut%27s_expedition_to_the_Land_of_Punt_by_%CE%A3%CF%84%CE%B1%CF%8D%CF%81%CE%BF%CF%82.jpg

13 Hans Bernhard (Schnobby), CC BY-SA 3.0 <https://creativecommons.org/licenses/by-sa/3.0>, via Wikimedia Commons: https://commons.wikimedia.org/wiki/File:Punt2.JPG

14 CvZ, CC BY-SA 4.0 <https://creativecommons.org/licenses/by-sa/4.0>, via Wikimedia Commons: https://commons.wikimedia.org/wiki/File:240911_CvZ-Palermo-stone.jpg

15 https://commons.wikimedia.org/wiki/File:Egypt_1450_BC.svg

16 https://commons.wikimedia.org/wiki/File:Hatshepsut_temple5.JPG

17 Zossolino, CC BY-SA 4.0 <https://creativecommons.org/licenses/by-sa/4.0>, via Wikimedia Commons: https://commons.wikimedia.org/wiki/File:2015-09-22-081415_-_Terrakotta-Armee,_Grosse_Halle.jpg

18 Thomas Lessman (Contact!), CC BY-SA 3.0 <https://creativecommons.org/licenses/by-sa/3.0>, via Wikimedia Commons: https://commons.wikimedia.org/wiki/File:East-Hem_400bc.jpg

19 Ji-Elle, CC BY-SA 3.0 <https://creativecommons.org/licenses/by-sa/3.0>, via Wikimedia Commons: https://commons.wikimedia.org/wiki/File:Sculpture_nok-Nigeria_(1).jpg

20 https://commons.wikimedia.org/wiki/File:Africa_Nok_Male_Figure_Kimbell.jpg

21 Werner Hammer, CC BY-SA 2.5 <https://creativecommons.org/licenses/by-sa/2.5>, via Wikimedia Commons: https://commons.wikimedia.org/wiki/File:San_wh03.jpg

22 https://commons.wikimedia.org/wiki/File:San-Paintings_Murewa_ZW.jpg

23 Yathin S Krishnappa, CC BY-SA 4.0 <https://creativecommons.org/licenses/by-sa/4.0>, via Wikimedia Commons: https://commons.wikimedia.org/wiki/File:Taurotragus_oryx_-_young_bull_-_Etosha_2015.jpg

24 https://commons.wikimedia.org/wiki/File:Samuel_Daniell_-_Kora-Khokhoi_preparing_to_move_-_1805.jpg

25 https://commons.wikimedia.org/wiki/File:Baines1848.jpg

26 Christian Manhart, CC BY-SA 3.0 IGO <https://creativecommons.org/licenses/by-sa/3.0/igo/deed.en>, via Wikimedia Commons: https://commons.wikimedia.org/wiki/File:Archaeological_Site_of_Carthage-130237.jpg

27 Damian Entwistle, CC BY-SA 2.0 <https://creativecommons.org/licenses/by-sa/2.0>, via Wikimedia Commons: https://commons.wikimedia.org/wiki/File:Carthage_National_Museum_representation_of_city.jpg

28 ArchaiOptix, CC BY-SA 4.0 <https://creativecommons.org/licenses/by-sa/4.0>, via Wikimedia Commons: https://commons.wikimedia.org/wiki/File:Carthago_-_350-250_BC_-_silver_tetradrachm_-_female_head_-_lion_and_date_palm_-_Berlin_MK_AM.jpg

29 GIRAUD Patrick, CC BY-SA 2.5 <https://creativecommons.org/licenses/by-sa/2.5>, via Wikimedia Commons: https://commons.wikimedia.org/wiki/File: Tunisise_Carthage_Tophet_Salambo_04.JPG

30 Franzfoto, CC BY-SA 3.0 <https://creativecommons.org/licenses/by-sa/3.0>, via Wikimedia Commons: https://commons.wikimedia.org/wiki/File:Garma_(Garama)_-_Ruinen_der_antiken_Stadt_Garma_02.jpg

31 Cattette, CC BY 4.0 <https://creativecommons.org/licenses/by/4.0>, via Wikimedia Commons: https://commons.wikimedia.org/wiki/File:Kingdom_of_Numidia-02.png

32 https://commons.wikimedia.org/wiki/File:Numidian_cavalry.png

33 (Public domain: https://commons.wikimedia.org/wiki/File:MASSINISSA_-_MAA_23_-_87000716.jpg)

34 https://commons.wikimedia.org/wiki/File:Giambattista_Pittoni-Sophonisba.jpg

35 No machine-readable author provided. Numidix assumed (based on copyright claims)., CC BY-SA 3.0 <http://creativecommons.org/licenses/by-sa/3.0/>, via Wikimedia Commons: https://commons.wikimedia.org/wiki/File:Tomb_of_Massinissa_01.jpg

36 https://commons.wikimedia.org/wiki/File:Jugurthine_war_Numidia-en.svg

37 https://commons.wikimedia.org/wiki/File:Mauretania_et_Numidia.jpg#file

38 Zil, CC BY-SA 3.0 <https://creativecommons.org/licenses/by-sa/3.0>, via Wikimedia Commons: https://commons.wikimedia.org/wiki/File:Juba_II_of_Numidia_burial_place.jpg

39 Newslea Staff, CC BY-SA 4.0 <https://creativecommons.org/licenses/by-sa/4.0>, via Wikimedia Commons; https://commons.wikimedia.org/wiki/File:Kingdom_of_Aksum_Map.png

40 Classical Numismatic Group, Inc. http://www.cngcoins.com, CC BY-SA 3.0 <http://creativecommons.org/licenses/by-sa/3.0/>, via Wikimedia Commons: https://commons.wikimedia.org/wiki/File:Ousas.jpg)

41 A. Davey from Where I Live Now: Pacific Northwest, CC BY 2.0 <https://creativecommons.org/licenses/by/2.0>, via Wikimedia Commons: https://commons.wikimedia.org/wiki/File:The_North_Stelae_Park,_Axum,_Ethiopia_(2812686646).jpg

42 I, Ondřej Žváček, CC BY-SA 3.0 <http://creativecommons.org/licenses/by-sa/3.0/>, via Wikimedia Commons: https://commons.wikimedia.org/wiki/File:Rome_Stele.jpg

43 Jialiang Gao www.peace-on-earth.org, CC BY-SA 3.0 <http://creativecommons.org/licenses/by-sa/3.0/>, via Wikimedia Commons: https://commons.wikimedia.org/wiki/File:Church_Our_Lady_Mary_Zion_Axum_Ethio.jpg

44 Marco Schmidt[1], CC BY-SA 3.0 <https://creativecommons.org/licenses/by-sa/3.0>, via Wikimedia Commons: https://commons.wikimedia.org/wiki/File:Cola_MS_6687.JPG

45 Musée du quai Branly, CC BY-SA 3.0 <https://creativecommons.org/licenses/by-sa/3.0>, via Wikimedia Commons: https://commons.wikimedia.org/wiki/File:Statuette_f%C3%A9minine-R%C3%A9gion_de_Djenn%C3%A9-Mali.jpg

46 Raymbetz, CC BY-SA 3.0 <https://creativecommons.org/licenses/by-sa/3.0>, via Wikimedia Commons; https://commons.wikimedia.org/wiki/File:Calendar_aswan.JPG

47 LassiHU, CC BY-SA 4.0 <https://creativecommons.org/licenses/by-sa/4.0>, via Wikimedia Commons: https://commons.wikimedia.org/wiki/File:Gebel_Barkal.jpg

48 LassiHu, CC BY-SA 3.0 <http://creativecommons.org/licenses/by-sa/3.0/>, via Wikimedia Commons: https://commons.wikimedia.org/wiki/File:Gebel_Barkal_Amun_temple_(B500).JPG

49 Dagelf, CC BY-SA 4.0 <https://creativecommons.org/licenses/by-sa/4.0>, via Wikimedia Commons: https://commons.wikimedia.org/wiki/File:Dunes_at_Tassili_n%27Ajjer.jpg

50 https://commons.wikimedia.org/wiki/File:Cave_painting_from_the_Tassili_n%27Ajjer_mountains.jpg

51 JialiangGao www.peace-on-earth.org, CC BY-SA 3.0 <https://creativecommons.org/licenses/by-sa/3.0>, via Wikimedia Commons: https://commons.wikimedia.org/wiki/File:Tellem_Dwelling_Bandiagara_Escarpment_Mali.jpg

52 I, Mgiganteus, CC BY-SA 3.0 <http://creativecommons.org/licenses/by-sa/3.0/>, via Wikimedia Commons: https://commons.wikimedia.org/wiki/File:Great_Mosque_of_Gede.jpg

53 Franzfoto, CC BY-SA 3.0 <https://creativecommons.org/licenses/by-sa/3.0>, via Wikimedia Commons: https://commons.wikimedia.org/wiki/File:Sabratha_-_B%C3%BChnenhaus_des_Theaters_2._Jh..jpg

54 joepyrek from Richmond, Va, USA, CC BY-SA 2.0 <https://creativecommons.org/licenses/by-sa/2.0>, via Wikimedia Commons: https://commons.wikimedia.org/wiki/File:Leptis_Magna_(29)_(8288918733).jpg

55 NH53, CC BY 2.0 <https://creativecommons.org/licenses/by/2.0>, via Wikimedia Commons: https://commons.wikimedia.org/wiki/File:Arch_of_Septimius_Severus,_Leptis_Magna12.jpg

www.ingramcontent.com/pod-product-compliance
Lightning Source LLC
Chambersburg PA
CBHW070335010526
44107CB00004B/513